AN ILLUSTRATED HISTORY C
WEAPONS
WORLD WAR ONE

A comprehensive chronological directory of the military weapons used in World War One, from field artillery and machine-guns to the rise of U-boats and Allied submarines

Covers the weaponry of both the Allied and Central Powers, with specification boxes providing information on each technology, and over 180 photographs

Ian Westwell

southwater

This edition is published by Southwater,
an imprint of Anness Publishing Ltd
Blaby Road
Wigston
Leicestershire LE18 4SE

Email: info@anness.com

Web: www.southwaterbooks.com; www.annesspublishing.com

Anness Publishing has a new picture agency outlet for images for
publishing, promotions or advertising. Please visit our website
www.practicalpictures.com for more information.

Publisher: Joanna Lorenz
Editorial Director: Helen Sudell
Editor: Elizabeth Young
Proofreading Manager: Lindsay Zamponi
Production Controller: Bessie Bai

Produced for Anness Publishing by Toucan Books:
Managing Director: Ellen Dupont
Editor: Donald Sommerville
Project Manager: Hannah Bowen
Designer: Elizabeth Healey
Picture Researcher: Debra Weatherley
Maps: Julian Baker

© Anness Publishing Ltd 2011

Previously published as part of a larger volume, *The Complete Illustrated
History of World War I*

PUBLISHER'S NOTE
Although the advice and information in this book are believed to be
accurate and true at the time of going to press, neither the authors nor
the publisher can accept any legal responsibility or liability for any errors
or omissions that may have been made.

ETHICAL TRADING POLICY
At Anness Publishing we believe that business should be conducted in an
ethical and ecologically sustainable way, with respect for the environment
and a proper regard to the replacement of the natural resources we employ.

As a publisher, we use a lot of wood pulp in high-quality paper for
printing, and that wood commonly comes from spruce trees. We are
therefore currently growing more than 750,000 trees in three Scottish forest
plantations: Berrymoss (130 hectares/320 acres), West Touxhill (125
hectares/305 acres) and Deveron Forest (75 hectares/185 acres). The forests
we manage contain more than 3.5 times the number of trees employed
each year in making paper for the books we manufacture.

Because of this ongoing ecological investment programme, you, as our
customer, can have the pleasure and reassurance of knowing that a tree is
being cultivated on your behalf to naturally replace the materials used to
make the book you are holding.

Our forestry programme is run in accordance with the UK Woodland
Assurance Scheme (UKWAS) and will be certified by the internationally
recognized Forest Stewardship Council (FSC). The FSC is a non-
government organization dedicated to promoting responsible management
of the world's forests. Certification ensures forests are managed in an
environmentally sustainable and socially responsible way. For further
information about this scheme, go to www.annesspublishing.com/trees

Front cover clockwise from top left: *Disabled FT-17 tank on the muddy
battlefield around St. Mihiel during World War I; Battle of the Somme, France,
1916, German soldiers preparing to throw hand-grenades from a trench near
Chemin Des Dames; June 1915; An Italian dreadnought battleship in action off the
Dalmatian coast; German soldiers firing a six-inch gun at an English Observation
post in Africa during World War I; German machine gunners wearing gas masks
during a gas attack.* Back cover: front flap, tl, br, 2, 66–7: *A German military
submarine has surfaced in the sea;* back flap, tmr, bmr, 3, 48–9 *Fixing bombs to
a biplane during World War I;* bl, 1 *A French tank heads to the front during
World War I;* bml, 3 *German troops advance through smoke and fire during the
first of Ludendorff's great spring offensives in 1918;* tr, 6–7 *British Mark IV
tanks and soldiers moving towards the front lines, France, 1918.*

Contents

Introduction

World War I was the first truly total global conflict, a titanic struggle between the then leading world powers for the domination of Europe and other areas that they had colonized in the 19th century. Even with such high stakes, the outbreak of the conflict was greeted with considerable popular enthusiasm in many – if not all – quarters. After years of sabre-rattling and accelerating arms races as well as intensifying economic and geopolitical rivalries, it was thought, not just by militarists, that a short, sharp war would bring a new stability to world affairs.

Like most wars, World War I turned out in ways that the participants did not anticipate at the outset. Almost everyone thought that the war would be short, a matter of months at the most. Economic and industrial developments were believed to have made it impossible for fighting to continue for long. In fact the reverse was true. Industrialization and mass production meant that armies of previously unequalled size could be supplied and kept fighting – leading to a casualty toll never before seen.

Military leaders struggled to cope with the consequences of the scale of the fighting and the new technologies involved – it was the first major war of aircraft, tanks, submarines, quick-firing artillery, poison gas and much more. It is hardly surprising that generals sometimes failed to make best use of these novel resources, but few were the stupid and unfeeling blunderers of popular belief.

When World War I ended after more than four years of bitter combat, in which the outcome was in doubt until the final stages of campaigning, few were really able

Below: People everywhere welcomed the outbreak of the war. These young Berliners have been called up to serve in the German Army, 1 August 1914.

Right: Belgian infantry manning trenches near Uskub (now usually called Skopje) in 1915.

to comprehend the sheer scale of the destructive events they had witnessed. Empires had toppled, new countries had emerged and the United States had been transformed into an international colossus. Despite the heavy loss of life, the victors could at least console themselves with the thought that they had won "the war to end all wars" – the popular rendering of the title of H. G. Wells's overly optimistic 1914 book entitled *The War That Will End War*. Yet the peace they had secured at such immense cost was transitory and was destined to last just two decades.

The new technologies that emerged during the war lead to important innovations in the development of military weaponry. This expertly written work brings together all the main weapons that were introduced and used during the war. Divided into three chapters, Army Weapons, Airforce Weapons and Airships, and Naval Weapons, the key weapons used during the war by the Allied and Central Powers are described. Listed chronologically, each features information explaining what each weapon is, how they worked, the successes and failures, and the tactics that often decided the outcomes. All these elements combine to form a detailed history of the technologies and weapons of World War I and give an in-depth analysis on how the war was fought.

Below: British troops blinded by poison gas wait for medical attention. Every major army was using gas by 1918, though this form of warfare would have been considered barbarous only a few years before.

ARMY WEAPONS

During World War I many new weapons were introduced by the armies of the Allied and Central Powers. This chapter examines all the key weapons, from British and German infantry men rifles and the first use of chlorine gas during the Battle of Ypres to the huge artillery of the Paris Gun.

Image: British Mark IV tanks and soldiers moving towards the front lines, France, 1918.

Heavy Artillery

Big guns were very much in short supply in every theatre of war during the first years of the conflict but they became the most important weapons in every country's arsenal once the fixed defences of trench warfare had developed.

The general lack of heavy artillery in 1914 partly reflected the recent experiences of the various warring nations. The French were still wedded to the idea of fast-moving warfare in the Napoleonic style of the early 19th century while the British had recently fought the elusive horse-mounted Boer commandos in the Second Anglo-Boer War (1899–1902). Neither saw the need for much more than highly mobile and rapidly deployed horse-drawn field artillery that could keep up with both infantry and cavalry.

GUNS AND FORTRESSES

The German and Austro-Hungarian planners had learned some lessons from the Russo-Japanese War (1904–5) in which the Japanese deployed heavy howitzers. Nevertheless, their armies marched to war in 1914 with a preponderance of field guns, though both of their general staffs expected to have to deal with enemy fortresses and knew they needed some heavy artillery. Prussian troops had been involved in sieges during the Franco-Prussian War and had found themselves short of the appropriate firepower. The response of the French to defeat in that war was to build or modernize a series of fortresses that might slow the fast movement of troops that Germany's Schlieffen Plan required. And Belgium, through

Below: A British (152mm) 6in gun position on the Western Front in 1917. This weapon fired a 45kg (100lb) shell to 12,500m (13,700yds).

which German troops would have to pass, had followed France's lead. Austria-Hungary had two potential major enemies – Russia and Italy – and war against either might involve fighting in the natural fortresses of the Carpathian Mountains and the Alps. In both cases shells with a plunging trajectory would be needed.

60-POUNDER GUN

This British weapon was introduced in 1905 and was the standard "heavy" gun serving with British divisions at the start of the war. It remained in use throughout the conflict but by the later years had been reclassified as a medium weapon and supplemented by much heavier designs.

CALIBRE: 127mm (5in)
GUN WEIGHT: 4,470kg (4.3 tons)
GUN LENGTH: 4.29m (14.06ft)
SHELL WEIGHT: 27.2kg (60lb)
MUZZLE VELOCITY: 634m/sec (2,080ft/sec)
MAXIMUM RANGE: 11,250m (12,300yds)

Above: An Austro-Hungarian Skoda-built 30.5cm (12in) "Schlanke Emma" howitzer in action.

Austria-Hungary led the way with Skoda's "Schlanke Emma" (Skinny Emma) a 30.5cm (12in) howitzer, while Germany's Krupp developed a 42cm (16.5in) weapon nicknamed "Dicke Bertha" (Big Bertha). Their combat debut was against Liège, supposedly the world's strongest fortress complex, on 12 August 1914. To the relief of the Germans and to the shock of their opponents, a dozen or so Emmas and Berthas reduced the city's supposedly impregnable concrete-and-steel fortresses to rubble in a mere four days.

As the trench lines were dug along the Western Front in late 1914, all of the combatants began fully to appreciate the need for heavy artillery to smash barbed wire, crumble trenches and bury deep dugouts in what was a new form of siege warfare, and they set about building such guns in large numbers or redeployed them from the now redundant fortresses. Little more than

eight per cent of France's artillery was of the heavy types in 1914, for example, but the figure was close to 50 per cent only four years later.

INCREASING FIREPOWER
Vast numbers of different heavy artillery pieces were developed. Some were moved around on wheeled carriages but others were transported in sections and placed on reinforced beds for firing. Some types like the French Army's 220mm (8.7in) Schneider Model 1917 could fling a 90.7kg (200lb) shell out to 22,400m (24,500yds) but most of the heavy howitzer types had shorter ranges. There was a simple trade-off – the heavier the shell, the shorter the range. The overall trend was for heavier, more destructive shells. The shell of the standard German field howitzer in 1914 weighed just 6.8kg (15lb), while that of the 21cm (8.3in) Lange Mörser (Long Mortar) of 1916 was a hefty 113kg (249lb).

KRUPP 21CM MORTAR/HOWITZER

Commonly referred to as the Long 21cm Mortar, this heavy howitzer entered service in 1916. Early versions were fitted with a gun shield but these were dropped for the subsequent variants.

CALIBRE: 21cm (8.3in)
WEIGHT: 6,680kg (6.57 tons)
GUN LENGTH: 2.3m (7.55ft)
SHELL WEIGHT: 113kg (249lb)
MUZZLE VELOCITY: 393m/sec (1,290ft/sec)
MAXIMUM RANGE: 11,100m (12,150yds)

KRUPP 15CM FIELD HOWITZER

This gun made its service debut in 1913 but Krupp produced an updated model, the FH17, during World War I. It actually differed little from its predecessor, except that it was somewhat lighter due to shortages of certain raw materials. The gun remained in German service for training until World War II.

CALIBRE: 15cm (5.87in)
WEIGHT: 2,200kg (2.17 tons)
GUN LENGTH: 2.1m (6.9ft)
SHELL WEIGHT: 42kg (92.6lb)
MUZZLE VELOCITY: 365m/sec (1,197ft/sec)
MAXIMUM RANGE: 8,500m (9,300yds)

Field Artillery

Light-weight, quick-firing, field artillery guns drawn by horses were the dominant and most numerous form of artillery at the outset of the war but their importance gradually declined in favour of heavier weapons with bigger shells.

Field artillery consisted of light horse-drawn guns that could keep pace with infantry and cavalry. They were allocated at the divisional level while the distribution of heavier, slower guns was the preserve of higher formation commanders. There were two main types of field artillery – *guns* that fired a high-velocity round on a comparatively flat trajectory, mostly against targets in the open and in the firer's line of sight, and *howitzers* that lobbed a lower-velocity round on an arcing trajectory to strike targets hidden behind cover. Both types could be identified by the diameter of the barrel's bore, the usual system on the European mainland, or alternatively by

the approximate weight of the shell they fired, a practice largely confined to Britain. Thus the field gun most widely deployed by the French in 1914 was the Model 1897 75mm (2.95in) while batteries supporting the British infantry relied on the Mark I 18-pounder (3.3in /84mm calibre) and the cavalry supports relied on the lighter 13-pounder (2.95in/75mm).

RATES OF FIRE

Most guns were quick-firers, capable of firing several rounds a minute. The best of these was the famous French "Soixante-Quinze" ("75"), the field gun that pioneered a recoil system in which only the barrel and not the whole carriage moved when

fired. The "75" was phenomenally quick-firing, with a well-trained crew able to get through up to 25 rounds a minute. The crew of the not dissimilar British 18-pounder could manage only eight a minute.

Similar guns were deployed by the other combatant nations. Germany, for example, relied on the 7.7cm (3.03in) field gun, a weapon widely exported to its allies, while Russia deployed the 76.2mm (3in) M1902. Whatever the gun type, field artillery guns usually weighed

Below: British 18-pounder field guns, photographed around the Belgian town of Ypres in late 1914, with their limbers and ammunition caissons close at hand.

roughly 900–1,350kg (2,000–3,000lb). The various field guns and howitzers had a maximum range of 6,500–8,000m (7,100–8,800yds), but under battlefield conditions targets were usually engaged at shorter ranges, often at least a third less than the

Above: Russian M1902 76.2mm (3in) field guns in action at the start of the war on the Eastern Front.

THE FRENCH "75" FIELD GUN

This was a revolutionary weapon when it appeared in 1897. It was light and highly mobile but most important of all it had a novel recoil system which meant that only the barrel and not the whole gun recoiled when fired. It therefore did not need to be re-laid on a target and a well-trained crew could fire an amazing 20-plus rounds in a minute. The 75 was really designed for fast-moving offensives and played a much lesser role in trench warfare.

CALIBRE: 75mm (2.95in)
GUN WEIGHT: 1,160kg (2,560lb)
GUN LENGTH: 2.7m (106in)
SHELL WEIGHT: 7.24kg (15.9lb)
MUZZLE VELOCITY: 530m/sec (1,735ft/sec)
MAXIMUM RANGE: 8,500m (9,300yds)

absolute range. There were variations in the number of guns in individual batteries but most countries deployed four. British cavalry and infantry divisions were the exception with six-gun batteries.

SHELL TYPES

There were two types of shell in service with field artillery. Shrapnel rounds, a largely anti-personnel weapon, were filled with metal balls and a bursting charge that was detonated by a preset time fuse ideally when in flight just above the enemy. High-explosive rounds had an impact fuse, which detonated when the shell hit the ground or another hard target such as a building. The force of the blast could destroy inanimate objects while both the detonation and splinters from the shell's ruptured casing were lethal to troops. Such rounds might fail to detonate if they struck soft or muddy ground.

Field artillery was essentially a weapon of mobile warfare and as such its importance on the Western Front declined with the advent of trench warfare. Shrapnel was ineffective against troops in cover and the high-explosive rounds fired by field guns were too light to make any impression on deep, strongly constructed dugouts. Despite their lack of firepower, field guns appeared in considerable numbers on the Western Front throughout the war. Improved fuses introduced later in the war meant that field guns could blast barbed-wire defences effectively. The British bombardment that preceded the opening of the Battle of the Somme in 1916 involved some 1,600 artillery pieces of which around 1,200 were either field or slightly larger medium guns. When the Germans launched Operation Michael, the first of their great offensives in 1918, they had 6,473 guns available; 3,965 were 7.7cm (3in) or 10cm (4in) field guns.

Rifles and Bayonets

The infantryman's rifle with its bayonet was the most ubiquitous weapon of the entire war and both were produced in their millions, but they were not the biggest killers – that "honour" went to machine-guns and, above all, artillery.

The rifle was the most commonly used weapon of World War I and, despite there being a sizeable number of manufacturers across Europe and beyond, all designs in service were largely similar in their mechanism and specifications. All were bolt-action, most of the straight-pull type, and all came with a magazine that allowed several shots to be fired without reloading. Some rifles had removable magazines but most were actually part of the rifle and the firer simply slotted clips of cartridges into them when reloading.

Rifles came in a rather limited variety of calibres. For example, the German Mauser Model 1898 had a calibre of 7.92mm (0.312in), while the Russian Moisin-Nagant was 7.62mm (0.3in) and the Romanian Mannlicher Model 1893 was 6.5mm (0.256in). British rifles were all 0.303in (7.7mm), while US types, like the Model 1903 Springfield, were 0.3in calibre. Most rifles were around 1.25m (50in) long and weighed some 4kg (9lb).

MAGAZINES

Most rifles had a magazine with a five-round capacity but some, especially British and French models, could take somewhat more. The French Lebel Model 1916, for example, had an eight-round magazine, while both the British Lee-Enfield Mark I and the SMLE (Short Magazine Lee-Enfield) Mark III had a detachable ten-round magazine. Both designs reflected the British Army's belief that rapid fire would shatter an attack and its regular infantrymen were able to achieve 15 or 20 aimed shots per minute over short periods. (Most armies considered rapid fire to be 8 or 12 rounds a minute.) The Lee-Enfield's bigger, clip-fed magazine and the rifle's turn-down bolt handle were incorporated into the design to aid quick firing. Hastily trained wartime soldiers could not match the pre-war regulars' standards of speed or marksmanship, however.

Below: British recruits take part in bayonet drill. This was considered an important part of training but bayonets killed very few soldiers.

Right: A good study of a British soldier on campaign. He is armed with an SMLE (Short Magazine Lee-Enfield) rifle, first introduced in 1907.

EFFECTIVE RANGES

Rifles were generally sighted up to as much as 2,560m (2,800yds) but most armies did not expect individual aimed fire to hit a specific target above 550m (600yds), a distance known as close range. Beyond this lay further zones as defined by the British Army – effective range at 600–1,400 yards (550–1,280m), long range at 1,400–2,000 yards (1,280–1,830m) and distant range at 2,000–2,800 yards (1,830–2,560m). Massed rather than individual targets could be hit at a rifle's effective range but it was not really worthwhile engaging anything at long or distant ranges.

BAYONETS

There were three main types of bayonet. The most common were the ones shaped like the blade of a knife, while others were thinner needle types that were prone to snapping, and the comparatively rare knife bayonets with a serrated blade that were mostly used by the Germans. Allied propaganda claimed the serrated edge was

GERMAN RIFLES

German infantry had two main types of rifle: the Mauser Gewehr 88 and the Mauser Gewehr 98 – first made in 1888 and 1898. The Gewehr 98 was exceedingly accurate and continued in German use until World War II.

CALIBRE: 7.92mm (0.312in) (Mauser Gewehr 98)
MAGAZINE: 5 rounds
SYSTEM: front-locking turn-bolt
LENGTH: 125cm (49.25in)
WEIGHT: 4.3kg (9.5lb)
MUZZLE VELOCITY: 870m/sec (2,854ft/sec)

deliberately designed to inflict even more horrendous wounds but it was actually for certain pioneering tasks.

Pre-war training manuals stressed the importance of the bayonet charge and most soldiers were inculcated with what the British termed the "spirit of the bayonet". The reality was somewhat different. Charges were extremely rare after 1914 and comparatively few people were killed or wounded by a bayonet thereafter. Bayonets were, of course, still used in trench fighting but an individual soldier faced with one was more likely to flee or surrender than fight it out. Detailed information on the precise number of bayonet wounds inflicted during the war is unavailable but it was undoubtedly extremely low compared with the big killer – artillery. British medical staff included bayonet wounds in their miscellaneous injuries category, which accounted for little more than one per cent of all casualties recorded by the British Army in the war.

SNIPING

Sniping was a valuable tool throughout the war, more so than in any previous conflict, and became especially important when static trench warfare developed. Snipers often worked as part of a two-man team with the other man being a target spotter equipped with binoculars or, more commonly, a trench periscope that protected him from enemy snipers. Snipers operated from camouflaged hides or behind metal plates with a rifle-sized slit cut into them to avoid being targeted themselves.

Right: A posed photograph of a German sniper, who would normally take up a much less exposed position.

Gas Warfare

Gas was deployed in considerable quantities during the war by most of the combatant nations and, although it became lethal and could produce truly horrible injuries, it was never a war-winning weapon.

Gas had been considered as a weapon before the outbreak of war but there was a general consensus that it was wholly "uncivilized". Yet all that changed with trench warfare, a development that sparked a wide-ranging search for technologies that could break the deadlock. Gas became acceptable and the types used changed from mere irritants with only short-term medical impact to ones with almost immediate lethality. Most were not long-lasting on the battlefield but a few were.

FIRST USES

The Germans were the first to use gas on the battlefield close to Neuve Chapelle on the Western Front in October 1914 and next in January 1915 near Bolimov on the Eastern Front.

Below: German stormtroopers undergo realistic training by advancing through a cloud of gas.

Above: British artillerymen pose for a photograph while preparing gas shells for use.

The amount of gas used was small and the results were not promising. At Neuve Chapelle the small quantity of the irritant gas released was not noticed by the targeted French troops while at Bolimov the xylyl bromide, a form of tear gas, froze due to the cold weather and therefore did not disperse. Nevertheless, the Germans persevered and introduced much more dangerous gases and these did have a significant effect.

Chlorine gas, which destroys the respiratory organs in a few seconds, was used to devastating effect during the Second Battle of Ypres in April 1915.

In the war as a whole Germany was the greatest user of gas (68,000 tonnes), while France manufactured 37,000 tonnes and Britain 25,000 tonnes.

Left: British troops blinded by gas in April 1918 await medical treatment and evacuation to the rear.

Below: Three early respirators, including a German Rahmenmaske (framework mask) and its carrying can (left).

TYPES OF GAS

The most widely used types were the aforementioned chlorine gas and the almost odourless mustard gas, a slow-acting agent that causes internal and external bleeding and vomiting and frequently leads to death. Some proponents of gas warfare concluded that lethality was neither necessary nor desirable. They reasoned that gas casualties who survived with considerable infirmity were a constant drain on medical facilities and detrimental to enemy morale in the long term.

Gas was dispersed in two ways. It was released in vapour form by fixed canisters positioned in or near the front line, a technique that wholly relied on the wind blowing in the right direction and one that meant that gas was effectively a short-range weapon. Artillery shells filled with an agent in liquid form that evaporated after a small explosive charge burst the shell open were widely used from 1916. Gas was also put in high-explosive rounds in small quantities for a "mixed" effect.

Artillery shells gave gas greater range and much better accuracy, but some problems still remained insoluble.

Gas was not a truly effective weapon as it needed a long list of ideal conditions. It often failed due to adverse weather, especially the strength and direction of the prevailing wind and the temperature. It was quite common for gas to be blown back into the attackers' faces by contrary winds.

All sides quickly developed gas masks and these became more and more sophisticated.

Early ones consisted of thick cotton pads soaked in bicarbonate of soda, to cover the mouth and nose, and separate goggles, but these gave way in all armies to the more familiar combined mask and respirator types. Filters were usually filled with charcoal or chemicals to neutralize the gas.

Below: Both men and animals needed protection against gas attack. The British Army began issuing horse respirators in 1916.

Trench Systems

Trench warfare developed on the Western Front in late 1914 and, although types of trenches varied considerably largely due to the impact of the local terrain, they became progressively deeper, wider and more complex as the war continued.

Trench systems were to some extent a reflection of local conditions, and the continuous lines most associated with the war were by no means their only form. In very mountainous terrain, as on much of the Italian Front or, indeed, in the Vosges region of France, the lines were generally less complete and might consist of a series of mutually supporting mountain-top strong-points. Not all trench systems were below ground but might rather be built up. This could be because the bedrock was near the surface and too difficult to dig through or the water table might be too near the surface so that sunken trenches would be waterlogged. This was

Below: Trench systems everywhere were plagued by rats and hunting them down was a task performed on a regular basis by all sides.

true especially on the most northerly part of the Western Front in Belgium, where there was a high water table and the Belgians had deliberately flooded much of the low-lying area near the coast in 1914.

Trenches evolved as the war progressed. They were originally little more than connected scrapes in the ground and not designed for permanent occupation but, once the fronts had become static in late 1914, the defence systems became deeper and more complex. The Germans – probably the most skilled exponents of trench building – began digging second trench lines from late 1915 and a third was added thereafter.

TRENCH LAYOUTS

The most typical type of system consisted of three lines about 730m (800yds) apart connected

by communication trenches. The first line, the one nearest the enemy, was the fire trench, the main line of resistance; the second was the support trench; and the third was the reserve. All trenches usually zigzagged or had angular firebays to minimize the impact of shellfire and prevent an enemy from firing directly down them. Dugouts, either deep underground or just shelters cut into the trench sides, were constructed to give troops even greater shelter and a measure of comfort. Sandbags were added for more protection, wooden shoring placed to prevent the sides from collapsing, and duckboards laid to aid drainage. Repair work to dug-outs was needed on an almost constant basis.

DEEPER DEFENCES

Although this system held good for much of the war, it did change and the lines became more complex from 1916 onward, when the Germans adopted "defence in depth". The line nearest the enemy consisted of relatively modest defensive outposts – strong-points based on large shell-holes or prefabricated concrete pill-boxes – that were not designed to stop an enemy advance but rather delay him or channel him into more exposed "killing zones". Next, up to 1.5km (1 mile) away, came the front line. Again this was not necessarily continuous but a system

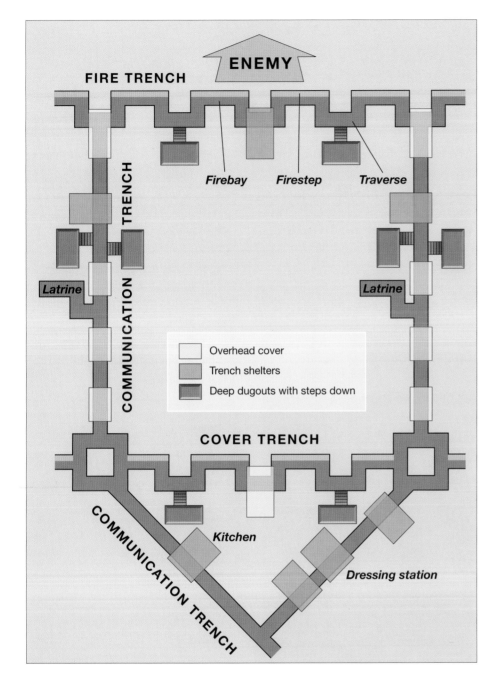

ENEMY

FIRE TRENCH

Firebay *Firestep* *Traverse*

COMMUNICATION TRENCH

Latrine *Latrine*

Overhead cover

Trench shelters

Deep dugouts with steps down

COVER TRENCH

COMMUNICATION TRENCH

Kitchen

Dressing station

SAPPING

This was a technique used to approach an enemy position without being exposed to fire. Small, narrow trenches, or "saps", were first dug out into No Man's Land and at a certain point the diggers would turn towards each other, thus creating a new trench line. Individual saps were also used as listening posts, particularly by the British who had a philosophy of dominating No Man's Land. Sapping was a tried-and-trusted technique but it was extremely slow and involved much back-breaking work.

The most formidable example of defence in depth was the Hindenburg Line, which ran along the northern and central sector of the Western Front. It was begun in September 1916 and was still under construction in late 1918. It actually comprised a number of large, mutually supporting fortified positions that had a depth of up to 16km (10 miles).

of mutually supporting strong-points that could be fired into from the rear if captured. Next came what was known as the "battle zone", an area perhaps 2km (1.2 miles) wide that consisted of a maze of short trenches and numerous strong-points capable of all-round defence. Behind this was the beginning of the "reserve zone" which might include yet more defensive trench systems and hold prepared emplacements for the artillery.

A TYPICAL TRENCH SYSTEM
A standard three-line trench system of the sort used on every war front.

Below: Some of the dense rows of barbed war that protected the German Hindenburg Line.

Mortars

Trench mortars, a type of specialist artillery that could fire explosive shells in a high trajectory, were not new, having been around for centuries, but the stagnation of trench warfare saw them become one of the most important weapons of the war.

Mortars are short-range infantry-support weapons designed to lob shells in a high arc on to a target. They were originally designed in the 18th century to hit targets sheltering behind either natural features such as hills or constructed defences like fortress walls. Although they had fallen out of fashion somewhat before World War I, several armies soon recognized that they were ideal weapons for hitting enemy troops sheltering in trenches. Germany, France and Britain were the major manufacturers and sold their various designs to their allies.

Below: British armourers prepared a huge number of "toffee apple" rounds for the early type of 2in (51mm) mortar, as seen here.

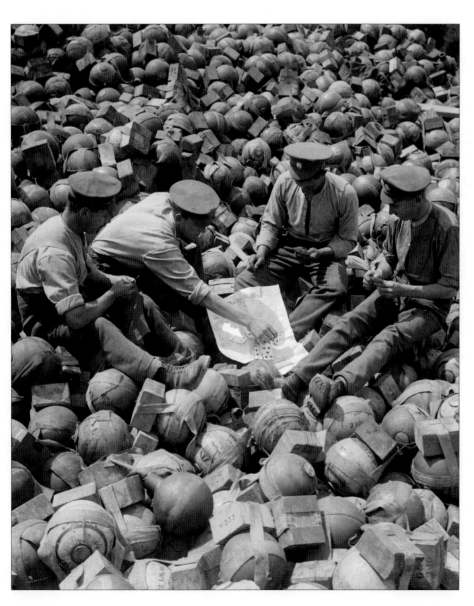

9.45IN MORTAR

As the war progressed Britain deployed a wide-range of mortars including the 9.45in type, seen here being loaded with its large projectile, commonly known as the "Flying Pig". Although very effective, these heavier mortars were difficult to manhandle around the battlefield.

TYPE: Heavy smoothbore mortar
CALIBRE: 9.45in (240mm)
WEIGHT: 866kg (1,910lb)
MAXIMUM RANGE: 1,600m (1,750yds)
CREW: 9

GERMAN SUPERIORITY

The Germans had the edge in the quality and provision of mortars for much of the early part of the war, largely because they had recognized that these weapons had played an important part in the siege warfare of the Russo-Japanese War. Consequently, the German

Army had a number of excellent *Minenwerfer* (mine-thrower) types from the outset. Around 150 had been delivered by August 1914. They were bigger, heavier and less portable than later mortars, largely because they had been designed specifically to take on the concrete and steel of France's frontier fortresses. They used a propellant charge to fire a variety of ammunition – explosive, incendiary and gas – that had a range of around 1,000m (1,100yds). Rifling made them quite accurate and their range was increased in later models by lengthening the barrel.

MINENWERFER

The smallest of Germany's late war *Minenwerfer* types is pictured here being pulled by part of its crew. All three calibres had wheeled carriages, which were usually removed before the weapon was used in action.

TYPE: Light rifled mortar
CALIBRE: 76mm (3in)
WEIGHT: 100kg (220lb)
MAXIMUM RANGE: 1,000m (1,100yds)
RATE OF FIRE: 20rpm
CREW: 6

They came in a variety of calibres, defined as light, medium and heavy, that fired projectiles weighing 4.08kg, 49.44kg and 95.26kg (9lb, 109lb and 210lb) respectively. The mortars were not really man-portable in the modern sense as most were very heavy. As they could not be broken down into various parts, they were moved about on two-wheeled carriages (the larger types normally horse-drawn) from which they could be fired if required but they were usually found mounted on a steel plate in the trenches. The Germans did attempt to resolve their mobility problem by introducing much smaller *Granatenwerfer* (grenade-thrower) types. These fired a finned grenade out to ranges of 230–275m (250–300yds) and were much lighter.

ALLIED DESIGNS

France and Britain had no modern mortars in 1914. The French resorted to bringing ancient ones out of retirement while the British experimented with contraptions that would not have looked out of place at a medieval siege. Some looked like miniature siege engines; others were large crossbows, such as the British Leach that could lob a small grenade up to 180m (200yds). One early design of 2in (51mm) calibre fired a bomb that looked like a large toffee apple.

True mortars began to arrive in 1915. The French developed the Batignolles, a series of heavy mortars. Arguably the best and certainly the most modern-looking mortar of the war was the British Stokes design. It was named after its

STOKES MORTAR

The British Stokes mortar could be easily moved by its crew. It was eventually made in 4in (101mm) and 6in (152mm) versions in addition to the most usual 3in calibre.

TYPE: Light mortar
CALIBRE: 3in (76.2mm)
WEIGHT: 49kg (108lb)
MAX. RANGE: 730m (800yds)
RATE OF FIRE: 22 rounds/min
CREW: 2

Above: An Australian-crewed 3in Stokes Mortar in action in a captured trench near Villers-Bretonneux in July 1918.

creator, Sir Wilfred Stokes, and began to appear in 1916. These came in a variety of calibres and fired a rocket-shaped grenade. Like all British and French mortars they were smoothbore designs. These were truly man-portable as they broke down into three sections – barrel, baseplate and adjustable bipod.

Machine-guns

Machine-guns, which were used both defensively and offensively, were among the most effective weapons of the whole conflict. There were relatively small numbers in use in 1914 but all armies had many thousands by the end of the war.

Modern machine-guns were developed in the second half of the 19th century. They equipped all armies in 1914 and appeared in ever greater numbers as the war progressed. The reason was simple – a heavy machine-gun fired 400–600 rounds a minute and could effectively fulfil the tasks of 80 or more rifle-armed infantry. Heavy machine-guns were mostly associated with defensive roles, in which they would fire on attacking infantry from a fixed position in a trench but they were also used offensively. Gunners were trained to elevate their guns so that the bullets would fly over the heads of advancing infantry and then gravity would bring the rounds down on an enemy target.

The weapon usually came in three parts – a mounting tripod or sledge, the weapon itself and a reservoir of water in a can that fed into the "water jacket" that surrounded the barrel and stopped it overheating. Some guns, like the French 1914 Hotchkiss and the American Colt, were air-cooled but that system was the exception rather than the rule. Bullets were fed into a machine-gun by strips of 30 rounds or, more commonly, longer woven or metal belts.

CUMBERSOME IN ACTION

Such bulky weapons were as difficult to manhandle as their name suggests. Most weighed 32–40kg (70–90lb), excluding the copious amounts of ammunition needed to keep the weapon firing. A British Vickers heavy machine-gun might have 16 250-round ammunition belts each weighing 10kg (22lb) available for immediate use and many more rounds in reserve.

MASCHINENGEWEHR 08

This weapon, introduced in 1908, was the mainstay of the German Army's heavy machine-gun detachments throughout the war in one form or another and was a very potent weapon indeed. Estimates suggest that it was responsible for around 90 per cent of the 60,000 or so casualties the British suffered on the first day of the Battle of the Somme in July 1916.

CALIBRE: 7.92mm (0.312in)
RATE OF FIRE: 600rpm
MUZZLE VELOCITY: 823m/sec (2,700ft/sec)
AMMUNITION: 250-round belt
WEIGHT WITH MOUNT: 56kg (124lb)

Left: A Russian M1910 "Sokolov" Maxim machine-gun and crew. The gunshield protecting the firer was not a common design feature.

VICKERS MARK I

The Vickers was based on the 1884 Maxim, the world's first automatic machine-gun, and entered service with the British Army in 1912. It was lighter than the original Maxim and was known for its reliability.

CALIBRE: 0.303in (7.7mm)
RATE OF FIRE: 500rpm
MUZZLE VELOCITY: 682m/sec (2,240ft/sec)
AMMUNITION: 250-round belt
WEIGHT WITH MOUNT: 33kg (73lb)

The average machine-gun needed two or three men to fire it, but most guns were operated by a team of four to six, the rest of whom carried ammunition. Soldiers often lugged heavy machine-guns around in battle but out of action they were broken down and transported by mules or placed on carts.

LIGHT MACHINE-GUNS

The war also saw the development of an entirely new type of weapon, the man-portable light machine-gun that could be easily carried so that the user could keep up with attacking infantrymen. They generally weighed 10–14kg (22–30lb), most nearer the former figure than the latter, could fire 250–600 rounds per minute under ideal conditions and were air-cooled. Light machine-guns were either belt- or magazine-fed but magazines proved more practical in battle. Germany produced the Maschinengewehr 08/15, essentially a stripped down version of the Maschinengewehr 08 heavy machine-gun fitted with a pistol butt and bipod, while France had the Chauchat, which remained the French Army's standard light machine-gun throughout the conflict. Something like 250,000 of them were manufactured and they saw service with many Allied forces, including the US Army, which purchased some 34,000 in 1917. Although the Chauchat was very light it was notoriously unreliable due to frequently poor manufacturing standards.

The best light machine-gun of the war was the Lewis, a US design from 1911 which was manufactured in Belgium and Britain. It was quite a heavy weapon and was difficult to lug across a battlefield but it did become the most common infantry support gun in the Belgian and British Armies. It was also highly adaptable and was fitted to aircraft, armoured cars and tanks.

Right: The French Hotchkiss was introduced in 1900 and the first air-cooled version arrived in 1914. The original strip magazine held a mere 30 rounds and was replaced by a 249-round metal belt from 1915.

Trench Warfare Weapons

Trench warfare demanded a whole new range of both fighting skills and specialist weaponry and the latter were often types that could be used at close quarters, not least hand grenades and the very earliest sub-machine-guns.

The need to clear trenches led to the development of specialist equipment. Troops required weapons that were less cumbersome and more lethal at close quarters than rifles and bayonets. Aside from improvised weapons, such as the coshes, clubs, knuckle-dusters and broad-bladed knives used in night-time trench raids, other weapons were developed through official channels.

Grenades were important in trench fighting as they allowed the thrower to attack an enemy without exposing himself to their fire. Yet, with the notable exception of Germany, many nations were slow to introduce them. The British authorities proved especially lax and

Below: Although the Germans were mostly associated with the stick grenade, the early years saw a great deal of improvisation until standard designs entered service.

Above: A late war German stormtrooper throws a standard Stielhandgranate (stick grenade) towards an enemy outpost while his colleagues take cover.

soldiers at the front improvised grenades out of tin cans, bits of metal for shrapnel, some form of explosive charge and a fuse. There was eventually a plethora of official designs but the most successful mass-produced types were the hand-thrown German Stielhandgranate (stick grenade) and more common "pineapple" design, such as the British Mills bomb, which found favour with both the Allies and Germany. Grenades could also be fired from a rifle with a cup adaptor slipped into its barrel.

FLAMETHROWERS

Germany also developed two wholly new weapons. The flamethrower was first tested in

ANTI-TANK TACTICS

When the first British tanks appeared in 1916, they terrified the German troops they attacked, many of whom simply fled. However, the Germans soon developed techniques and weapons to counter the armoured threat. Trenches were made wider, thereby becoming effective anti-tank ditches. In 1918 the Germans also introduced "tank forts", which consisted of two field guns located in a forward position protected by several machine-guns and infantry. These weapons – artillery was the biggest tank killer – could take on tanks at close range as could flamethrowers, as illustrated here. The Germans also developed specialist anti-tank rifles and a special type of bullet that could penetrate a tank's armoured plate.

Flamethrowers were actually more of a psychological than a practical weapon and were very vulnerable when used offensively. Because of their short range they had to get very close to their objective, which was no easy feat as their carriers were invariably targeted before they got to close quarters.

SUB-MACHINE-GUNS

The Germans also used the world's first sub-machine-gun – the 9mm (0.345in) Bergmann Maschinenpistole 18/1 – a type of weapon that was ideal for trench fighting. Production began in early 1918 but did not really get into its stride until the middle of the year by which time the Germans were totally incapable of major offensive operations. Nevertheless, it was a basically sound design, light enough to be used in attack, but its 32-round magazine did have teething troubles. It certainly worried the Allies – they put a clause in the Treaty of Versailles prohibiting its manufacture.

Germany in 1901 and during World War I it came in both portable and non-portable versions. The latter was effectively static and solely of use defending trenches but the former was more practicable for clearing enemy positions. Both types used an oil and petrol mix projected out of a pipe by a gas such as nitrogen. Fuel and propellant were stored in a cylinder and ignited by a burning taper attached to the pipe's nozzle.

There were two types of German flamethrower. The Kleif (Kleinflammenwerfer – "small flamethrower") was a cumbersome device needing a crew of two, one of whom carried a fuel container the size of a milk churn on his back and the

other who aimed and fired the weapon. The more readily manageable Wex was operated by one man who carried the fuel in a lifebelt-like container on his back. The Kleif had a range of some 25m (27yds) and the Wex about 20m (22yds).

The French developed the Schilt, which was named after its creator, a captain in the Paris fire service. It had more fuel than its German counterparts so it could fire up to 10 bursts of flame out to 30m (32yd). The British devised two types of portable flamethrower, the Norris-Menchen and Lawrence, but they were never used in action save for a small version during the raid on Zeebrugge in 1918.

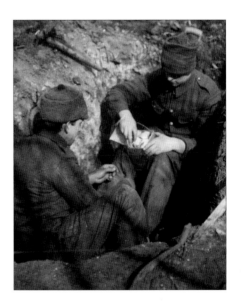

Above: British soldiers improvising grenades using tin cans filled with gun cotton, scrap and a basic fuse.

British Tanks

The British developed the first truly viable tank at the beginning of 1916 and, while they did score some noteworthy successes, they were generally too underpowered and overly prone to mechanical failure to reach their full potential.

The first tanks, tracked armoured vehicles fitted with some form of armament, were developed in Britain but the concept only emerged slowly and involved many different agencies and individuals. Although the gestation period was prolonged, the design moved swiftly from prototype to production to battle. The prototype, nicknamed Mother, first ran in January 1916 and was rhomboid in shape with two side-mounted "turrets", commonly known as sponsons.

Production of the Tank Mark I began in April and they went into action on 15 September during the Battle of the Somme.

Their attack initially went well, literally scaring the Germans out of their trenches, but thereafter their effectiveness diminished rapidly. Due to the appalling conditions inside their armoured cabs, crews were soon left sick and disorientated; many tanks also broke down

due to mechanical failure and others simply bogged down in muddy trenches and shell craters. Nevertheless, they had done sufficiently well for more to be ordered.

MALES AND FEMALES

Tanks became available with different combinations of weapons. "Males" carried a pair of light artillery guns and four machine-guns and "Females" were armed with six machine-guns. The most widely used tank of the war was the Mark IV. The first of these arrived at the front in April 1917. There were 595 Female Mark IVs and 420

NAMING THE TANK

It may seem curious but the tank's complex development was partly the responsibility of the Royal Navy, mostly because First Lord of the Admiralty Winston Churchill was a backer of the project. As a result, the first tanks were actually known as His Majesty's Landships. It soon became apparent that the name potentially gave away the nature of the top secret weapon to an enemy with an imagination that was vivid enough. A less obvious codename was thus needed, and various suggestions were made, each reflecting its shape. Cistern, container and reservoir were all suggested but tank quickly became the preferred option.

Below: The Mark A Whippet was, as its name suggests, an attempt to create a fast-moving medium tank to exploit any breakthrough but its top speed was still only 13kph (8mph).

Left: Mark V tanks, here fitted with trench-crossing cribs, made their debut in July 1918. They had slightly thicker armour and more powerful engines than earlier types.

Males, but a number of the former were converted into "Hermaphrodites" by replacing the right-hand sponson with a Male sponson with its mix of machine-guns and a light gun.

As the capabilities and limitations of tanks became better understood, they underwent various modifications and improvements. So that they could cross the wider trenches the Germans had dug in part as tank traps, "Tadpole Tails", extensions to the rear of the tank, were tried but proved to be too flimsy so designers much more successfully turned to extending the main body itself. It was, however, more common for tanks to carry fascines on their roofs that could simply be rolled into a trench, thereby making a bridge for them to cross. Early versions were bundles of logs and brushwood held together by chains, but later ones consisted of a steel crib. Tanks were often thwarted by the mud and shell craters of No Man's Land so they were given "ditching gear", essentially a wooden beam that could be drawn under the tracks to give greater purchase, or their tracks' width was extended with plates to spread the load.

FASTER DESIGNS

As the value of tanks became clear, the British developed a faster light tank that was supposed to work with cavalry and exploit any breakthrough made by the heavier tanks. The first Medium Mark A, more commonly known as the Whippet, was built in October 1917 and they went into action for the first time on 26 March 1918.

Tanks were neither as good as their exponents believed or as bad as their detractors argued. They made significant advances in the first days of the tank-led Battle of Cambrai in late 1917 but had performed woefully amid the mud of Passchendaele. However, they were never able to make a decisive break-through and then keep the momentum of the attack going. This was largely due to their mechanical unreliability.

TANK MARK I

The Mark I was the first tank to go into action. Some 49 were deployed and enjoyed a degree of local success but most were soon knocked out by enemy fire or broke down.

WEIGHT: 28.5 tonnes
CREW: 8
MAX. SPEED: 6.5kph (4mph)
MAX. ARMOUR: 12mm (0.47in)
ARMAMENT: 2 x 6pdr (57mm) and 4 machine-guns (Male)

French and German Tanks

*Both the French and Germans produced their own armoured fighting vehicles
during the war. France put three types of tank into service but Germany built just
one model and instead often relied on tanks captured from the British.*

The French were the keenest supporters of armoured warfare after the British. There was no one driving force behind their programme and the two Allies' tank plans evolved along largely separate lines. French armoured cars had been of some military worth before the arrival of trench warfare and a few enlightened figures in the Ministry of War believed that vehicles that could operate off-road might break the stalemate on the Western Front. The key figure was a colonel of artillery, Jean-Baptiste Estienne, who proposed a tracked armoured fighting vehicle to the general responsible for weapons procurement in December 1915. Estienne's concept was suitably impressive and an order for 400 *chars d'assaut* (assault vehicles) was issued on 31 January 1916.

FIRST FRENCH DESIGNS

Schneider was the first company to be given a procurement order and soon came up with a box-like armoured superstructure

mounted on a chassis developed from a US Holt tractor. The vehicle weighed some 13 tonnes and had a top speed of less than 6.5kph (4mph). There were endless delays in production, largely because of shortages of armour plate. The first Schneider reached the army on 8 September 1916 but only seven more had arrived by late November, the date when all 400 should have been built. As Schneider was clearly struggling

Above: A St Chamond tank is camouflaged in the factory before delivery to the French Army in 1917.

to fill its order from an early stage, St Chamond, a design company, was asked to fulfil a second order for 400 tanks in April. Its prototype was not dissimilar to the Schneider but was nearly 70 per cent heavier.

Neither tank performed well in action. Their high profile made them vulnerable to

---

RENAULT FT-17

The French FT-17 was the first tank to have a revolving turret and was designed in 1917. It had an adequate cross-country performance and saw service with both the French and US forces on the Western Front throughout 1918.

WEIGHT: 6.5 tons
CREW: 2
MAX. SPEED: 10kph (6mph)
MAX. ARMOUR: 16mm (0.63in)
ARMAMENT: 1 x 8mm (0.315in)
  machine-gun or 1 x 37mm
  (1.46in) gun

artillery fire, their engines were not overly reliable and, worst of all, their trench-crossing abilities were poor. Of the two, the St Chamond was the worse. Its greater weight meant that it was even more likely to sink into soft ground and its super-structure overhung the tracks substantially at the front, making it prone to getting stuck while crossing a trench.

Both types achieved little during their combat debut, the Nivelle Offensive in April 1917. A number remained in service for the rest of the war but they were largely superseded by a light tank, the Renault FT-17, from the end of 1917. This was a much lighter and smaller design used extensively during the later stages of the war by both the French Army and the American Expeditionary Force. The Renault had a good cross-country performance and its turret gave it an all-round field of fire but thin armour made it very vulnerable.

German Scepticism

The German High Command was not overly impressed with tanks, citing their high rate of mechanical failure and their vulnerability to anything from difficult terrain to artillery fire. A German-built type did reach the front from late 1917 onwards but production was limited due to the crippling shortage of raw materials.

The A7V Panzerkampf-wagen was by some way the biggest tank of the war. It had a

Right: The Schneider tank had poor ventilation and thin armour but worst of all its internal petrol tanks lacked adequate protection.

PANZERKAMPFWAGEN A7V

Germany's massive A7V entered service in late 1917 but had a high centre of gravity and inadequate engines that gave it a poor cross-country capability.

WEIGHT: 32 tons
CREW: 16
MAX. SPEED: 13kph (8mph)
MAX. ARMOUR: 30mm (1.2in)
ARMAMENT: 1 x 57mm (2.24in) gun; 6 x 7.92mm (0.312in) machine-guns

large box-like structure that housed a 16-man crew, while firepower was provided by a single forward-firing 57mm (2.24in) cannon and six heavy machine-guns. The A7V was ponderously slow, prone to mechanical failure and was so top heavy that it was likely to overturn if moved along a slope. Only a few dozen of them were ever built and they were easily outnumbered by the captured and refurbished British tanks that the Germans also used in the later stages of hostilities.

Mine Warfare

The detonation of huge caches of high-explosive under an enemy's front line was a common aspect of trench warfare and could be highly effective as the explosions not only destroyed defences but also often left any survivors too dazed to fight.

Early versions of modern land mines were developed during World War I but they were rather primitive devices. The Germans, for example, made extensive use of mortar bombs part buried in the ground as an early type of minefield to destroy tanks. Mine warfare usually had a rather different meaning during the conflict and referred to digging shafts under enemy trenches, filling them with high-explosive and then detonating the charges. It was dangerous work due to tunnel collapses, flooding, gas and the danger that the enemy might explode camouflets (counter-charges) to bury the tunnellers in their own shaft. Almost all the mine warfare of World War I took place on the Western Front as the static nature of the fighting gave tunnellers the time they needed to drive their shafts underground.

FIRST MINES

The Germans actually set off the first underground explosion of the war on 20 December

Above: A lone soldier gives some indication of the size of craters left by a mine detonation.

1914, when 10 out of 11 mines were detonated immediately beneath a brigade of Indian troops near Festubert, some 16km (10 miles) south of the Franco-Belgian border. However, the British became the war's greatest exponents of tunnelling but had no specialist units in existence in 1914. They

were actually the brainchild of a persistent member of parliament, John Norton Griffiths, who submitted the idea in December 1914. He had a contract to build sewers through the clay soil under a northern town and employed men known as "moles" who "clay kicked"

Below: A vast crater produced by the detonation of just one mine at the beginning of the Battle of the Somme in 1916.

or "worked on the cross". They sat in the tunnel with their backs supported on a wooden backrest (cross) with their feet pointed at the tunnel face and used them to work a spade-like implement to dig out the clay, which was then passed back for disposal. Alternative methods using mining machines were rarely tried and not successful.

Formal approval for the creation of specialist mining units was finally issued on 12 February 1915 and the first units were designated 170 to 178 Tunnelling Companies, Royal Engineers. The first recruits were British miners of every sort but companies were later also raised in Australia, Canada and New Zealand.

BRITISH ATTACKS

The first British mines were exploded under Hill 60 near St Eloi on the evening of 17 April and thereafter the operations grew larger and more complex. The biggest mining operation in military history reached fruition in mid-1917 but the idea had first been mooted as far back as 6 January 1916.

The target was Messines, a German-held ridge a little to the south of Ypres. The tunnellers planned 21 explosions in all and the charges were placed in 12 main shafts, some with two or more galleries leading off them, along a 16km (10 mile) stretch of the ridge. The building of the mines was an immense effort – one was over 640m (2,100ft) long. Once completed they were mostly filled with Ammonal, the most powerful explosive then known. One particular mine contained more than 43 tonnes and the tunnellers placed close to 430 tonnes of explosives under the German lines.

Nineteen mines in total were exploded on 7 July 1917 (two failed to go off) and the devastation caused was immense. The largest crater, Lone Tree, was 12m (40ft) deep and 76m (250ft) across. No one knows how many German troops were killed by the simultaneous detonations, which were heard in London and beyond, but some 10,000 men were recorded as missing on the first day of the battle. A further 7,350 were taken prisoner, many in a wholly dazed condition.

Below: German officers prepare to detonate a mine under the enemy trenches in the early part of the war.

Coastal, Fortress and Railway Artillery

Although most artillery weapons deployed during the war were mounted on wheeled carriages, other artillery pieces were either placed in fixed positions, such as fortresses, or, if especially large, on purpose-built railway mounts.

There was something of a mania across much of Europe for updating existing frontier fortresses or building modern versions of them in the decades before World War I. Austria-Hungary, Germany and Russia all built such fortresses but the greatest exponents were the French and Belgians. Theirs were generally built around strategic towns and cities, like Liège and Namur in Belgium or Verdun and Belfort in France, and comprised a number of outlying forts fitted with heavy artillery pieces and machine-guns. The artillery was positioned inside retractable steel domes in the most modern forts.

Above: The French, like the British and Germans, operated railway artillery. In this case, an improvised 155mm (6.1in) rail gun fires on a distant German position.

The frontier fortresses proved to be paper tigers as they could not withstand the newest and heaviest forms of artillery introduced before and during the war. After both supposedly impregnable Liège and Namur had fallen in a matter of a few days in August 1914, the French saw the writing on the wall and began to remove many of their fortress guns, mount them on field carriages or flatbed rail trucks and send them to the field army as it was especially short of heavier forms of artillery no matter how ancient.

COAST DEFENCES

Coastal artillery received a major overhaul in the second half of the 19th century largely due to the development of the armoured warship. Generally, the guns were placed in brick and earth and later concrete emplacements to protect important sections of the coast or key harbours, although lighter types

---

BRITISH BL 12-INCH RAIL GUN

The British built just two of these large rail guns initially (the guns themselves were originally designed for naval service). They were in France by late 1915 and two more went into action during 1916.

WEIGHT: 170 tonnes (approx)
CALIBRE: 12in (305mm)
WEIGHT OF SHELL: 340kg (750lb)
MUZZLE VELOCITY: 813m/sec (2,666ft/sec)
MAX. RANGE: 30km (18.5 miles)

---

were more mobile and might be placed behind extemporized defences. They were usually supported by various other weapons, such as machine-guns, searchlights and anti-submarine barriers. However, coastal artillery actually saw little action during the war, aside from occasionally replying to long-range fire from distant enemy warships, as amphibious assaults were extremely rare.

The British did keep their coastal artillery largely intact to combat any invasion threat and the Germans also used such types to protect certain bases. The island of Heligoland was heavily defended not least because it protected the seaways leading to the home ports of the High Seas Fleet. The German Navy was also particularly anxious to protect the entrance to the canals at Zeebrugge and Ostend on the coast of occupied Belgium as

they led inland to the U-boat base at Bruges. The coastal defences at Zeebrugge and Ostend were both tested by a British attack in April 1918 but they survived mostly unscathed.

RAIL GUNS

The heaviest guns deployed in the ground war were usually moved about on rail mounts so

Above: An armoured revolving artillery cupola in an Alpine redoubt, of the kind found in many fortresses of the era.

that they could be easily transferred from firing position to firing position by locomotives. Such guns were overwhelmingly deployed on the Western Front where there were usually excellent rail links not far behind the static battle lines. The first experiments were carried out by the French, who put redundant coastal or fortress guns on flatbed rolling stock during late 1914. Purpose-built rail guns began to appear later. The chief drawback with these types was that they had limited left–right traverse and thus had often to be moved about on a section of curved track to acquire a new target. Smaller calibre railway guns were commonly mounted in such a way that they could be traversed through 360 degrees.

Left: A captured German coastal battery in Belgium. These concrete emplacements offered very little protection for their crews.

Anti-aircraft Guns

There were very few anti-aircraft guns in existence in 1914 but with the rapid development of aerial warfare they soon became an important weapon in the battle for air supremacy and were deployed in their thousands.

No one had given much thought to the threat posed by aircraft in the years before World War I and, therefore, no one had given much thought to developing anti-aircraft guns to knock them out of the sky. Germany was the first country to demonstrate such weapons in 1908–9 and these, which were known as "balloon guns" and built by either Krupp or Rheinmetall, merely consisted of a field gun converted to fire at a high angle from a truck or large automobile. At the time there was a belief that these would actually be able to keep up with the slow-flying aircraft of the day. Other types, usually those positioned to defend targets like major cities, were essentially guns taken from their original carriages and placed on static angled mounts that could be turned through 360 degrees.

As there were so few aircraft around both before and at the outbreak of the fighting in

BRITISH 13-POUNDER

This anti-aircraft weapon was a combination of a light field gun used by British horse artillery batteries and a Thornycroft J-type lorry, one of the most ubiquitous petrol-engined vehicles of the war. It first saw service in 1915. A standard gun section was two such weapons accompanied by two other lorries for the crew, range-finding equipment and ammunition.

Shell weight: 5.9kg (13lb)
Gun weight: 975kg (2,150lb)
Elevation: +80 degrees
Vertical range: 4,000m (13,100ft)
Muzzle velocity: 520m/sec (1,700ft/sec)

Left: The crew of a German anti-aircraft machine-gun await the order to open fire. Note the gun's very large ammunition drum.

August 1914, there was very little incentive to spend large amounts of money developing dedicated anti-aircraft guns. The British, for example, had no more than a handful of guns on towed mounts, while the French, who were even less prepared, had just two armoured cars based on the De Dion Bouton automobile that each carried a field gun fitted to a special high-angled mount in the rear for anti-aircraft work. Nevertheless, these autocannon were subsequently used extensively by the French and were also sold to Britain to bolster London's air-defence network in 1915–16.

MOBILE GUNS

Anti-aircraft guns in the field tended to be a marriage of an existing light or medium field gun placed on a high-angled mount and fitted to a flatbed truck or to a purpose-built carriage that could be towed by another vehicle. Thus, in one case, the British adapted a light field gun, a weapon normally associated with horse artillery batteries that fought alongside cavalry units. It was put on the back of trucks with drop-down sides, chiefly the Peerless Motor Lorry or the Thornycroft J-type. These were usually fitted with stabilizers and screw jacks to prevent the recoil of the gun from overturning them. Guns could typically be elevated between 70 and 90 degrees and their shells generally had a maximum altitude of around 4,000m (13,100ft), although some could reach higher.

FIRE CONTROL

The main problem for the anti-aircraft gunners was trying to hit a target that, although comparatively slow-moving, was effectively able to move in three dimensions. So if a gun was fired directly at the target then by the time the shell arrived at the right altitude, the target would have moved on. The gunners began dealing with the problem by fitting complex sights to their weapons but this was effectively a duplication of effort within a battery and it was found simpler to have what was known as a central post sight. This was positioned in the middle of a group of guns and, once its crew had worked out the necessary data of height, range and speed, the information was given to all of the guns.

In reality, the available anti-aircraft technology was very much in its infancy during the war and, while there are no firm figures of the number of aircraft downed by such batteries, it was overwhelmingly dwarfed by the number of aircraft shot down in combat by other aircraft. However, anti-aircraft fire could be of sufficient nuisance value to disrupt a reconnaissance or put a pilot off when making an attack.

Right: US troops man a French-built Hotchkiss heavy machine-gun deployed in the anti-aircraft role. This weapon's greatest weakness was the metal strip magazine that can be seen here as it held no more than 30 rounds and thus required frequent changing.

FRENCH 75MM ANTI-AIRCRAFT GUN

The French made extensive use of their famed 75mm (2.95in) gun in the anti-aircraft role, largely because of its high rate of fire. The weapon's wheeled carriage was simply removed and the gun mounted on a De Dion car fitted with several stabilizers, one of which is shown here in front of the rear wheel. Note also the rangefinder on the right.

SHELL WEIGHT: 7.16kg (15.8lb)
GUN WEIGHT: 4,000kg (8,800lb)
ELEVATION: +70 degrees
VERTICAL RANGE: 4,725m (15,500ft)
MUZZLE VELOCITY: 530m/sec (1,740ft/sec)

The Paris Gun

German troops pushed to within 160km (100 miles) of Paris in the spring of 1918 and this allowed them to deploy a pair of huge, technologically advanced artillery pieces to bring the French capital and its inhabitants under direct fire.

The Paris Gun was a huge artillery piece designed purely to fire on the French capital to undermine civilian morale at a time when the German Army was launching a series of offensives on the Western Front in March – August 1918. It was officially designated the Lange 21cm Kanone (Long 8.3-in Cannon) but was nick-named "Wilhelm's Gun" in honour of the German emperor.

Below: Test firing the "Paris Gun". Each shot wore the barrel away significantly so succeeding shells had to be a little larger until, after 60 shots, the barrel had to be changed.

The idea of the gun was first mooted in spring 1916, a time when some sections of the Western Front were "just" 96km (60 miles) east of Paris.

DESIGNING THE GUN

The project was masterminded by Krupp and a body known as Artillery Direction, part of the Imperial German Navy. Their work was exceedingly difficult, not least because of the weapon's complex ballistics, and it was made doubly so when German troops withdrew to the Hindenburg Line from autumn 1916, thereby increasing the distance to Paris by a further

20km (12 miles) or so. Never-theless, they pushed the project forward over the following months and finally conducted successful test firings of the weapon at their Mappen prov-ing ground. The ultimate design could be broken down into sections, transported by rail on specially produced carriages and then reassembled at the required point – but all this was an immense effort.

INTO ACTION

The bombardment of Paris was conducted from three positions to the north-east and east of the capital, all near various railway lines running around Laon and Reims and all in the middle of a forest. The work on these positions began in November 1917 and carried on into January and February 1918. Each required much preparation work – new track was laid, emplacements were dug and huge volumes of concrete made to create foundations sound enough to take the weight of the reassembled gun. Great efforts were also made to camouflage the various firing positions. The first of these was located at Crépy-en-Laonnois and was used 23 March – 1 May when 183 rounds were fired; the Bois de Corbie was used on two occasions, 27 May – 11 June (104 rounds) and 5–9 August (66 rounds); while the third position was used only briefly 15–19 July (14 rounds) at the Bois de Bruyères.

Thus, 367 shells fell on or near Paris during the various attacks, killing 256 civilians and wounding a further 620, but there was no set routine. More shells might fall on one day than the next, and several days might pass without any landing at all. This might have been because the gun's barrel needed replacing after just 60 rounds had been fired or because the gun was being moved. One thing

Below: A crowd of curious onlookers examines a little of the damage done by a round from the "Paris Gun".

did become clear on the second day of the bombardment. The previous day's shells had landed some 20 minutes apart but on the morning of 24 March two struck just three minutes apart, meaning that there were at least two Paris Guns in action.

The Paris Guns proved largely invulnerable and neither was ever destroyed by the Allies. Their bombardment only ended following the successful Allied counter-attacks in August that pushed the German line back so that the French capital was beyond their range. Some of the guns' emplacements were overrun but there was no sign of the weapons themselves. Nor was any trace of them ever found. The most likely explanation is that they were cut up and the high-grade metal put to other uses.

Ground-attack Aircraft

Close co-operation between ground and air units became a very important part of offensive operations during World War I but few dedicated aircraft were ever built and still fewer entered service before the later stages of the conflict.

Light bombers and fighters were commonly used for close-support missions during World War I infantry offensives but they were not as effective as dedicated ground-attack aircraft. Light bombers tended to drop their ordnance from medium altitude and would often be inaccurate, while fighters could strafe enemy positions with their machine-guns and drop small loads of bombs – but such low-level work was very dangerous and heartily detested by the majority of pilots. Both they and their unprotected aircraft were highly vulnerable to the huge volume of machine-gun and rifle fire that would greet them as they swooped down on a target. True ground-attack aircraft began to appear from 1917 onward and were usually, but not always, fitted with some form of armoured protection to improve the chances of their crews' surviving over the battlefield.

GERMAN DESIGNS

Germany's AEG company produced one of the first ground-attack aircraft, the J-type. It was introduced in 1917 and based on the company's C-type, a two-seater reconnaissance aircraft with an armoured engine. The J-type was given a more powerful engine and two downward-firing forward machine-guns. This design was only intended as a stop-gap measure until dedicated ground-attack aircraft appeared but production problems with the latter led the J-type to be used until the end of the war by which time some 600 had been built.

Another of the major German producers was Albatros, who introduced a two-seater, also known as the J-type, on the Western Front from late 1917. It was essentially a replacement for the AEG J-type and was based on the earlier Albatros C-type, which was primarily a two-seater reconnaissance/light bomber series that was also used for ground-support work. The Albatros J-I was by no means fast and had a reputation for being difficult to fly but it had some useful attributes. The designers had added armoured protection for the two-man crew and fitted the aircraft with three machine-guns of which two were positioned to fire down through the fuselage. The J-I's chief weakness in action was that its designers had neglected

Left: A close-up view of the rear gun position of a German AEG C-IV, a multi-purpose aircraft that performed ground-attack missions.

to protect the engine. This oversight was remedied with the J-II, which was introduced in 1918, but few had reached the front before the end of the war.

Two of the leading aeronautical designers of the day, Hugo Junkers and Antony Fokker, developed the Junkers J-1 two-seater biplane as a ground-attack aircraft. It was based on an all-metal prototype but was modified so that its rear fuselage was made of wood. The J-1 first flew in late 1917 and participated in the great German offensives of spring 1918. Its greatest assets were that it was popular with pilots and the crew had a radio so that it could be easily directed to a target by

SALMSON 2

This sturdy and agile aircraft entered service with the French in early 1918 and was also purchased by the United States Army Air Force. Despite the crew positions being rather far apart, which made communication difficult, it was a well-liked type and some 3,200 were built in total.

Type: Ground-attack, light bomber, reconnaissance
Engine: 260hp Canton-Unné
Crew: 2
Ceiling: 5,000m (16,400ft)
Top speed: 184kph (114mph)
Range: 500km (310 miles)
Armament: 3 x 0.303in (7.7mm) machine-guns, light bombs

JUNKERS J-1

The Junkers J-1 was an all-metal biplane designed by Hugo Junkers and it first entered service in early 1918. Some 227 were built jointly by the Fokker and Junkers companies before the end of the war. The aircraft was partially armoured and this extra weight necessitated longer take-offs and landings. It was also slow and clumsy in flight and somewhat difficult to handle

but it was popular with its crews for its robustness – especially in action at low levels.

Type: Ground-attack, air–ground liaison
Engine: 200hp Benz Bz.IV
Crew: 2
Ceiling: 4,000m (13,120ft)
Top speed: 155kph (96mph)
Armament: 3–5 x 7.92mm (0.312in) machine-guns

ground units. The biggest drawback was that the J-1 was rather difficult to build and only 227 had entered service by November 1918.

ALLIED RESPONSES

The Allies tended not to build dedicated ground-attack aircraft but relied more on multi-purpose types. The French, for example, introduced their Salmson 2 in early 1918 and it not only undertook ground-attack duties but also flew as a light bomber and conducted reconnaissance sorties.

Britain used its Sopwith F-1 Camel fighter for ground-support work but it suffered heavy losses because it lacked armoured protection and an attempt to produce the TF-1 (Trench Fighting 1) Camel came to nothing. The first true type was the Sopwith TF-2 Salamander, which went into mass production in May 1918 but saw little service.

Equipping the Americans

The United States had to build a mass army of hundreds of thousands from scratch. However, it lacked an industrial base that was geared up for war production to equip those troops, so it largely relied on Britain and France for its weaponry.

Britain and France had well-developed war industries by mid-1917 but were increasingly short of manpower due to the heavy casualties they had suffered in the preceding years. The United States, in contrast, had huge reserves of untapped manpower but largely lacked the wartime industrial base needed to equip them. Rather than wait for the Americans to clothe and arm their own armed forces, a time-consuming business at a point when speed was of the essence, it was thought better for Britain and France to provide US land and air forces with the means to fight the war. The US Navy, the country's strongest service, was fit to go to war and required no help from either Britain or France.

This decision on supply also meant that the shipboard space that would have been used to carry vast quantities of arms and equipment overseas was left

Above: US troops fighting in the Argonne make use of a French-built 37mm (1.46in) trench gun.

free to ferry greater numbers of US troops to Europe much more quickly. There was no doubt that this plan was a wise one as some two million US troops crossed the North Atlantic during 1917–18.

UNIFORMS AND RIFLES

US troops did largely go to war in their own uniforms and carrying home-produced small arms but there were exceptions even to this. The infantry mostly wore British steel helmets but troops serving with French formations, generally segregated African-American units, instead wore the French Adrian helmet.

CURTISS JN-4D "JENNY"

The Curtiss JN-4 was the most successful US aircraft of the war period but it was a trainer not a combat type. Nevertheless, this version, the first to be mass-produced, was used in large numbers and some 5,500 had been built by the end of 1918.

ENGINE: 90hp Curtiss OX-5
CREW: 2
CEILING: 3,000m (9,850ft)
TOP SPEED: 112kph (70mph)
ARMAMENT: none

American troops were equipped with US small arms, including the excellent 1903 Springfield Rifle and the Browning Automatic Rifle but they also used French and British weapons, including the Rifle M1917 (Enfield), derived from a British design, and the wholly French Chauchat light machine-gun. The African-American troops serving with the French were armed with the Lebel and Berthier rifles. The main heavy machine-gun deployed throughout the US Army was the US 1917 Browning.

ARTILLERY

However, when it came to heavy equipment the American Expeditionary Force (AEF) was overwhelmingly dependent on French and British designs. In the case of artillery the AEF relied mainly on the French 75mm (2.95in) field gun and 155mm (6.1in) howitzer. The British also supplied a number of 8in (203mm) howitzers. The

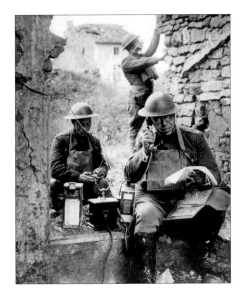

Left: A US communications detachment with a field telephone. Line repair was a constant task.

AEF's armoured force mainly consisted of French Renault FT-17 light tanks and its few heavier tanks were all British. There were plans to mass produce an "Allied" or "Liberty" tank based on the British Mark VIII design fitted with a US aero-engine at a plant in France but the war ended before it came into service.

The pilots of the United States Army Air Service largely earned their wings on US-built aircraft like the Curtiss JN series but they went into combat flying British and French designs, many of which were built under licence in the United States and fitted with US aero-engines. Others were simply bought from Britain and France; they had delivered 4,881 and 259 aircraft, respectively, by the war's end. The chief fighters flown by US squadrons were the French Nieuport 28 and various Spad S-types, while by later in 1918 the bomber units were mostly equipped with French Breguet 14 and Salmson 2 machines supported by a significant number of American-built DH-4s.

Below: Most of the American Expeditionary Force was equipped with foreign-built artillery, including the famous French 75mm (2.95in) field gun seen here in action.

Supply Transport

As befitted a highly industrialized war fought on a vast scale, World War I demanded the production of huge quantities of weapons and equipment and these were transported to the fronts by both long-established and much newer means.

The movement of men and equipment, indeed all types of military necessities up to the front, was a vital if unglamorous part of every country's military effort during World War I. Such items would be transported to the theatre of war by sea and rail, and then be moved by rail to stations usually some way behind the front where they would be unloaded and transported to large supply dumps. From these distribution points they would be sent forward to those who needed the particular supplies. The task of getting such quantities of supplies to the front was immense, virtually ceaseless and the rate

Below: A camel supply column, as used by the British forces during the campaign in Palestine.

Above: This shell dump gives a good indication of the huge quantities of all types of war material required to keep the armies fighting.

of consumption often huge, especially during major battles and offensives.

For example, on 5 September 1914, the first day of the Battle of the Marne, the French

had 465,000 rounds of 75mm ammunition stockpiled; five days later they had just 33,000 shells left. The British hit similarly high levels of consumption in 1916 – they fired more rounds in the week before the opening of the Battle of the Somme than they had in the previous 12 months. The Germans stockpiled some 1.16 million shells for their March 1918 offensive and fired virtually all of them in just five hours on the 21st.

FOREIGN LABOUR

Several of the combatants scoured the world for workers to keep an existing supply system going or expand it. Both Britain and France used labour drawn from their overseas colonies. Britain alone used more than one million porters from its own and various other African colonies during the war in East Africa but even this was not enough as the average soldier there required three porters. Even in Europe where the war was far less mobile, the supply network required huge numbers of labourers. China was a major contributor and by 1918 some 100,000 Chinese workers, both skilled and unskilled, worked in British labour corps on the Western Front, roughly the same number served with the French and a further 6,000 with the AEF.

ANIMAL POWER

World War I was largely powered by the horse. The official establishment of a British infantry division in 1914 included 877 vehicles and close to 5,600 horses, but only 9 motor cars, and matters had not changed much by 1918. The very same division was allocated 822 horse-drawn vehicles and some 8,840 horses but just 11 motor cars, 3 lorries and 21 motor ambulances. The need for horses and other animals, such as mules, camels and even bullocks, was all but insatiable and produced a terrible death toll. Some 542,000 horses died in French service alone during 1914–18, for example, and the British lost close to 485,000 horses and other animals.

Despite these figures, there is little doubt that motor transport did play a growing role in the supply chain. Trucks and a small light railway largely fuelled the French resupply effort during the titanic Battle of Verdun in 1916 and by June some 12,000 vehicles, at times one every 14 seconds, had

LIGHT RAILWAYS

The importance of narrow-gauge railways cannot be over-emphasized. Their tracks were usually just 60cm (2ft) apart and this made them much faster to build. The British Army, for example, estimated that a mile of light railway took 1,760–2,400 man-days to build while standard gauge took 4,300. Light railways were used by all sides and were pivotal in supplying the front line with every necessity. Some were also used to bring troops to within easy distance of the trench line.

Left: A British light railway pictured beside the River Scarpe – itself used as a supply artery – during the Battle of Arras in 1917. Water transport was often used to take wounded men to hospital as it gave a smooth ride.

moved up and down the *Voie Sacrée*, the only available road into the town.

Many of the original motor vehicles were simply civilian types pressed into service. The British, for example, converted around 1,300 buses belonging to the London General Omnibus Corporation into B Type Motor Lorries. Increasingly, however, major vehicle manufacturers, including such companies as Dennis, Leyland and Wolseley, began to supply purpose-built designs. A similar pattern was followed by the French Army, which requisitioned 1,049 civilian buses, 2,500 cars and 6,000 lorries in the final months of 1914, but thereafter Renault, Schneider and others began to supply appropriate vehicles.

Above: Motor transport, like these French trucks, was little used in 1914 but had become commonplace by later in the war.

Communications

All generals were dogged by the particularly thorny problem of communicating effectively with their troops at the front and, although various means were tried to overcome the long-standing difficulties, none was wholly satisfactory.

One of the greatest problems faced by any commanding officer in World War I was the difficulty in receiving progress reports and sending orders once a battle had begun. In most previous wars a general had been able simply to roam the comparatively small battlefields at will, seeing for himself what was happening and issuing and revising orders as required, but this was clearly impossible when the 1914–18 battlefields stretched over many miles and might involve much bigger forces. Consequently, commanding officers planned their attacks down to the smallest detail and issued step-by-step timetables for offensives so that every unit knew what it was to do and when. The problem was that battles rarely went to plan and it was difficult to respond to events quickly because of communication problems.

Most belligerents used wireless telegraphy for Morse code transmissions during the hostilities (speech transmission was not yet available) but it suffered two great weaknesses. First it could be intercepted by the enemy and even if the message was in code it might still be read. The Allies were fortunate enough to capture two sets of German naval codes in August 1914 and in one case the Germans did not realize the codebook was in enemy hands until 1918. The second problem was the wireless sets – they were bulky, heavy and fragile. Underpowered early aircraft, for example, could not take off with a wireless on board, while the sets could not long withstand the rigours of front-line service on the ground. Lighter, smaller and more robust models did become available as the war progressed and were commonly found in reconnaissance aircraft and balloons, but other means of communication remained in place on the ground.

TELEPHONE SYSTEMS

Once static warfare had developed the preferred method of communicating was either by voice or Morse code via telephone or buzzer but this had one major drawback – its vulnerability. Even though cables were often buried a metre or more below ground, they were repeatedly cut by artillery fire. Repairing such breaks was a difficult and dangerous occupation

Above: A German messenger dog captured in mid-air as it races to the rear to deliver a message.

Right: A US soldier mans a field telephone during the fighting in the Argonne in late 1918.

for the signallers whose duty it was to maintain the system. Matters were even worse once a battle had begun. Portable handsets existed but as their cables had to be laid on the surface of No Man's Land, an area undoubtedly under heavy artillery fire and often by both sides, there was a high probability that the cables would be cut.

LIVE MESSENGERS

More often than not attacking soldiers had to rely on other methods of sending and receiving messages but each had weaknesses. Written or oral messages were often sent by runner. This was arguably the most dangerous occupation on a World War I battlefield with a high probability of death or injury so that the message might never get through. It was also obviously much slower than transmission by telephone, especially if the runner got lost as many did. Carrier pigeons fulfilled a similar role and, although also highly vulnerable, could be effective. One played a pivotal role in the defence of Fort Vaux during 1916's Battle of Verdun and was posthumously awarded France's top award for gallantry.

There were other means of transmitting information but they were generally even more haphazard. Signal rockets were widely used in emergencies, often to call down artillery fire on pre-arranged co-ordinates, and the British even sewed reflective metal triangles on their back packs during the opening stages of the Battle of the Somme in 1916 so that the sun would glint off them and give those in reserve some idea of the troops' progress.

Above: Most of the major combatants deployed carrier pigeon units on the Western Front and the birds were housed in specially built lofts such as this impressive example.

Below: A pigeon is released from the interior of a British tank during the summer of 1916. Some animals were given decorations for their war service.

Pistols

Handguns were widely issued to troops during the war but were the main weapon carried by officers, partly as an indication of rank. They were useful weapons in confined spaces, such as trenches and vehicles of various sorts.

Revolvers and automatic pistols were the personal sidearms of officers of every rank, from the youngest second lieutenant to the most senior field marshal, and as such were as much a symbol of authority as a potentially deadly close-quarters weapon. There were other soldiers, some not necessarily of the officer class, who also made use of these weapons and this was in part because they operated in confined areas where it was considered impracticable to wield anything as long as a rifle. The types of troops in this category included airmen, tunnellers and, of course, tank and armoured car crews. The military police were also usually permitted to carry sidearms as they needed their hands free to check paperwork and manhandle troublesome prisoners if necessary.

PISTOL DESIGNS

There were three types of pistol available in 1914 – the common revolver that had a rotating chamber holding something like six rounds, and two types of clip-loaded automatics – recoil-operated and "blowback" designs. There tended to be a small number of major pistol manufacturers in each of the main combatant nations and they dominated production. Webley produced a staggering 300,000 of its Mark VI revolver for the British armed forces from 1915, for example, but even with that scale of output pistols were still sometimes in short supply and some less-known types were pressed into service as a stopgap. Britain, for example, made use of US Colt automatics which were largely distributed to the Royal Navy, the Royal Naval Air Service and the Royal Flying Corps.

Other nations also had favoured manufacturers. Luger is synonymous with German

pistols but Germany's armed forces also used smaller quantities of designs like the Mauser and Beholla automatics. All of these were also sold to both Bulgaria and Turkey, some 22,000 to the former alone. The armed forces of the other Central Power, Austria-Hungary, also used German designs but they also had their own 1911 Steyr automatic and other types. On the Allied side, the major

---

MAUSER AUTOMATIC

This weapon, probably the most powerful pistol to see service in the war, went into production in the 1890s and first found favour with the Italian Navy. During World War I it was deployed by the German armed forces but in a modified, re-calibred form from 1916.

FIRST ISSUED: 1894
CALIBRE: 7.63mm (0.3in)
MAGAZINE: 10 rounds
OVERALL LENGTH: 280mm (11in)
WEIGHT: 1.13kg (40oz)
MUZZLE VELOCITY: 440m/sec (1,444ft/sec)

STEYR M1911

The Austrian Steyr "Hahn" M1911 was a successful semi-automatic design and remained in military service until after WWII. It was renowned for its durability and ease of maintenance and was used by several countries.

FIRST ISSUED: 1911
CALIBRE: 9mm (0.354in)
MAGAZINE: 8 rounds
OVERALL LENGTH: 216mm (8.5in)
WEIGHT: 1.02kg (36oz)
MUZZLE VELOCITY: 361m/sec (1,185ft/sec)

---

sidearms' producers were Lebel in France, Glisenti and Beretta in Italy and Colt and Smith & Wesson in the United States. Belgium, Russia and Serbia either bought in pistols or built them under licence, although Russia did have some home-grown types available.

COMBAT USE

Pistols did have their uses, despite having a comparatively short range. They were effective in confined spaces and were of some value in trench fighting but more experienced and therefore possibly more wary officers often abandoned them as the war progressed. This was in part because they marked the wearer out as an officer, thus making it easier for the enemy to identify and neutralize him. An officer might prefer to make himself more anonymous by carrying a standard rifle.

However, the revolver or automatic pistol remained a potent signifier of authority throughout the conflict and the vast majority of officers continued to carry them into battle despite the potential risks.

The Luger was a 9mm (0.354in) weapon with a muzzle velocity of 350m/sec (1,150ft/sec)

The pistol had an overall length of 222mm (8.75in)

A seven-round clip of bullets was fitted into the butt.

Right: The Luger pistol was used by the German armed forces but was in fact a Swiss design from 1900 that was produced under licence from 1904 onward.

There is also no doubt that one particular blowback pistol, actually a Belgian-made seven-shot 7.65mm (0.301in) Browning Model 1900, played a key, indeed pivotal, role in World War I – it was the weapon used by 19-year-old Bosnian Serb nationalist Gavrilo Princip to assassinate Archduke Franz Ferdinand and his wife, Sophie, Duchess of Hohenberg, at Sarajevo on 28 June 1914.

WEBLEY MARK V

This weapon in several slightly different marks was arguably the most ubiquitous sidearm of the entire war. It was the standard British service pistol throughout the conflict and hundreds of thousands were produced.

FIRST ISSUED: 1913
CALIBRE 0.455in (11.4mm)
MAGAZINE: 6 rounds
OVERALL LENGTH 235mm (9.25in)
WEIGHT: 1.0kg (35oz)
MUZZLE VELOCITY: 180m/sec (590ft/sec)

Left: The Glisenti was a seven-shot 9mm (0.354in) Italian pistol that had an overall length of 216mm (8.5in) and had a muzzle velocity of 275m/sec (900ft/sec).

Armoured Cars

Armoured cars offered scouts a degree of protection and firepower that could not be easily matched by cavalry patrols but they were often fitted with under-powered and unreliable engines and were therefore not really suited to off-road action.

The first viable petrol engine and the first petrol-driven vehicle appeared in 1885 and the first recognizable armoured cars began to emerge in the period after 1902. As is the case with most new technologies, there was generally little standardization at first. Many of the designs were merely experimental or made from what resources were locally available, and only a handful or so ever saw action on the battlefield. Generally, they were built on chassis derived from civilian cars or light trucks and covered in armour plate of various thicknesses that gave them a boxy rather than streamlined shape. They might be fully enclosed or open-topped, and have one or more turrets, while armament ranged from light to heavy machine-guns and up to small-calibre cannon. Most ran on four

Below: Armoured cars in Russian service – a French-built Peugeot (foreground) and a Belgian Mors.

ROLLS-ROYCE ADMIRALTY PATTERN

This British-produced armoured car was based on the Silver Ghost civilian car and was used from late 1914 by the Royal Naval Air Service but the various squadrons were taken over by the Army in late 1915.

ENGINE: 40–50hp Rolls-Royce
TOP SPEED: 80kph (50mph)
CREW: 2–3
MAX. ARMOUR: 12mm (0.47in)
ARMAMENT: 1 x 0.303in
(7.7mm) Vickers Maxim

pneumatic tyres (with two driven wheels) but a small number made in Russia were half-tracked.

Armoured cars were mostly built by the car and truck manufacturers of the day, such as Minerva, Mors and SAVA (Société Anversoise pour Fabrication des Voitures Automobiles) in Belgium; Austin, Lanchester, Talbot, Wolseley and Rolls-Royce in Britain; Peugeot and Renault in France; Büssing, Daimler and Ehrhardt in Germany; and Fiat and Lancia in Italy. Some, especially British and Belgian designs, were produced in one country and exported to other Allied nations but it was not uncommon to find them being captured and used by the enemy. Germany used some British-built Austins taken from Russia, while Austria-Hungary deployed types captured from both Russia and Italy.

LIMITATIONS IN ACTION

Armoured cars only truly function during mobile warfare and they are used for reconnaissance and intelligence gathering, launching ambushes, outflanking the enemy, or pursuing a defeated foe. In World War I they served on most fronts, but were more common or saw more active service in some rather than others. This was partly due to the nature of the fighting. On the Western Front, they played an active role in the first stages

Right: A Belgian Minerva armoured car fitted with a single Hotchkiss machine-gun in action during 1914.

of the fighting in 1914 before the trench lines were dug and in the latter part of 1918 when operations once again became more fluid. Terrain and going also influenced their deployment. Many were heavy, underpowered and lacked traction so they were unsuitable for crossing hills, muddy ground or soft sand. One of the main problems was that the wheels of armoured cars were exposed, thereby making them vulnerable to enemy fire. Equally, the armour plate was effective against small arms fire but only beyond certain distances and was wholly ineffective against any type of artillery fire.

BRITISH DESIGNS

Britain led the way in wartime armoured car development in 1914 when a Royal Naval Air Service officer, Commander C. R. Samson, used cars largely sourced from around Dunkirk to rescue downed pilots and report on the movement of enemy troops and airships. Samson began by using poor-quality locally produced armour plate but then started requesting better materials from his superiors who in turn asked a number of British manufacturers to design purpose-built armoured cars. Austin eventually produced the most, many of which were earmarked for Russia, but Rolls-Royce undoubtedly made the best. The first three Rolls-Royce (Admiralty Pattern) types made their debut in December 1914 and both they and later models were sent to the fronts where the fighting was more mobile. They were especially active in the Middle East, serving with considerable success in both Palestine and Mesopotamia (Iraq).

PANZERKRAFTWAGEN EHRHARDT

The Ehrhardt was one of three types of armoured car in service with Germany from 1915 and was arguably the best. An updated version (pictured here), which appeared two years later, was little different except for the addition of armour plate over the headlamps and rear wheels.

ENGINE: 85hp Ehrhardt
TOP SPEED: 60kph (37mph)
RANGE: 250km (155 miles)
CREW: 8–9
MAXIMUM ARMOUR: 7mm (0.276in)
ARMAMENT: 3 x 7.92mm (0.312in) machine-guns

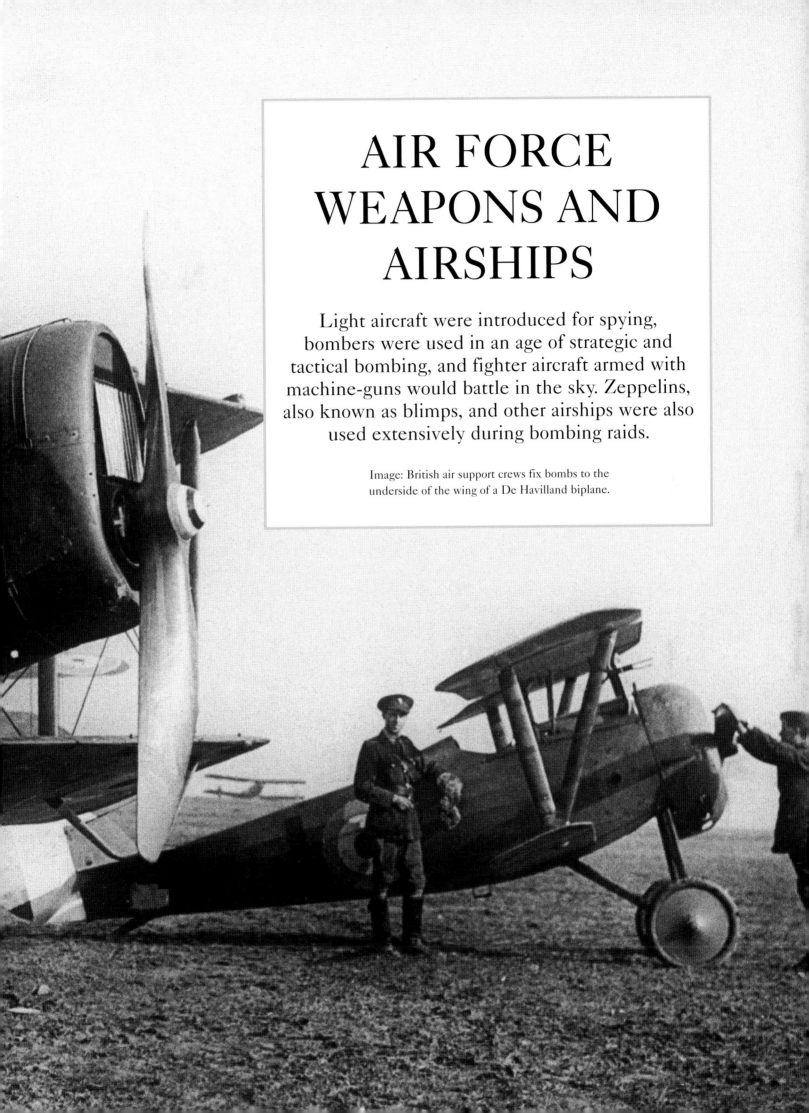

AIR FORCE WEAPONS AND AIRSHIPS

Light aircraft were introduced for spying, bombers were used in an age of strategic and tactical bombing, and fighter aircraft armed with machine-guns would battle in the sky. Zeppelins, also known as blimps, and other airships were also used extensively during bombing raids.

Image: British air support crews fix bombs to the underside of the wing of a De Havilland biplane.

Reconnaissance Aircraft

Aircraft technology was very much in its infancy at the outbreak of World War I but most combatant nations did possess a few reconnaissance aircraft and these types became ever more important once static warfare had begun.

Something like 19 out of every 20 aerial sorties flown throughout World War I were reconnaissance missions. There is no doubt that such aircraft played an increasingly key role in the conflict yet there had been considerable resistance to their introduction before the war – military aviation was still in its infancy in 1914 and many generals doubted its value.

THE NEW CAVALRY?

There were also comparatively few aircraft available in 1914; many country's air arms had only recently been founded; and most senior generals had little idea of what to do with them. Traditionally cavalry units were considered an army's eyes but aircraft soon proved their worth in reconnaissance. A German two-seat *Taube* monoplane played an important spotting role during the Battle of Tannenberg on the Eastern Front in late August 1914, for example, and these aircraft soon became indispensable when trench warfare reduced cavalry to immobility all along the Western Front.

Thereafter, reconnaissance aircrafts were deemed so important that fighter aircraft were developed specifically to shoot them down or protect them. They also became more and more sophisticated. Reports delivered in person or written and dropped gave way to immediate radio messages, while bulky hand-held cameras gave way to smaller types fitted with-

in the fuselage. Later versions were stripped of any extra weight, including weapons, to fly higher and faster. They became ubiquitous over every front – more than half of fighter ace Baron Manfred von Richthofen's 80 "kills" were of reconnaissance aircraft.

The first types had only to be stable platforms for observation and did not have to be fast or

Above: Part of the Western Front photographed from a reconnaissance aircraft. Commanders increasingly relied on photo-mosaics made up of many images like this when planning attacks.

FARMAN MF-11

These French-built "pusher" aircraft were designed by Maurice Farman and were in general service in 1914. They saw action with the British and the French and fought on every front before being withdrawn from combat in 1915.

TYPE: Reconnaissance/bomber
ENGINE: 80hp Renault
CREW: 2
CEILING: 3,000m (9,840ft)
TOP SPEED: 96kph (60mph)
ARMAMENT: 1 x 0.303in (7.7mm) machine-gun

NIEUPORT 12

Nieuport built several designs for the French Army during World War I including the Nieuport 10 reconnaissance biplane, which made its debut in 1915. This was soon super-seded by the Nieuport 12, enlarged and faster, and fitted with both rear- and forward-firing machine-guns. It was in service until early 1916.

TYPE: Reconnaissance/fighter
ENGINE: 110hp Clerget
CREW: 2
CEILING: 3,400m (11,150ft)
TOP SPEED: 160kph (100mph)
ARMAMENT: 1 or 2 x 0.303in
(7.7mm) machine-guns

manoeuvrable as there was little chance of them being downed until fighters appeared. Earlier "pusher" types like the French Farman MF series or the British FE-2a, could manage no more than around 88kph (55mph) and even tractor types, like the German Albatros B-I and B-II, struggled to get above 104kph (65mph). Most of these had no weapons but they began carrying both machine-guns and bombs from late 1914.

LATER DEVELOPMENTS

The newer types that appeared in subsequent years were far more advanced. Albatros, for example, produced a whole range of increasingly advanced armed reconnaissance aircraft, including the C-I to C-III series (1915–16) and the C-V to C-XII types (1916–18). The highly successful C-X carried both bombs and machine-guns and had a top speed of around 196kph (120mph). Germany had other manufacturers, such as Aviatik, who produced the C-1 to C-III series (1915–17), and Halberstadt, who produced the C series (1917–18). Their C-V and Rumpler's C-VII were fitted with radio and cameras, making them the first truly modern photo-reconnaissance aircraft, able to record enemy positions and spot targets for artillery batteries.

Allied designers kept pace with the enemy, producing aircraft like the French Nieuport 10 and 11 (1915–16) with top speeds of around 140kph (85mph) and 155kph (95mph). Some designers opted for multi-purpose aircraft that could perform a number of battlefield functions. The British had the Royal Aircraft Factory's RE-8 (1916–18), a mass-produced multi-purpose biplane that could also undertake bombing and ground-attack missions.

Above: The *Taube* ("Owl") mono-plane gained its name because of the bird-like shape of its wings. It was built both in Austria and Germany. Most were withdrawn from service by early 1915.

RUMPLER C-IV

The German company of Rumpler built many types of reconnaissance aircraft starting with the unarmed B-I, available in August 1914. This was replaced by the C-series, from early 1915. Hundreds of these were built, culminating in the C-VIIIR.

TYPE: Reconnaissance/bomber
ENGINE: 260hp Mercedes
CREW: 2
CEILING: 6,350m (20,800ft)
TOP SPEED: 170kph (105mph)
ARMAMENT: 2 x 7.92mm
(0.312in) machine-guns +
100kg (220lb) bombs

Early Fighters

The idea of arming aircraft to shoot down other aircraft only truly evolved in the first months of World War I, when it was soon recognized by air power advocates that reconnaissance aircraft were a vital weapon in modern warfare.

There were no purpose-built fighter aircraft in existence in 1914 but they were quickly developed once the trenches had been dug. Their first roles were to protect the increasingly important reconnaissance aircraft that had taken the place of redundant cavalry and to shoot down those of the enemy.

The earliest types, some of them monoplanes but mostly biplanes, were usually conversions of two-seater reconnaissance aircraft that had been fitted with a single machine-gun operated by the observer from the rear of the cockpit. The chief problem was that the machine-gun was easiest to aim when firing forward but most aircraft were of the "tractor" type. The propeller was at the front of the fuselage and there was no means of firing through its arc without shooting the wood to bits.

PUSHER FIGHTERS

There was one exception: "pusher" aircraft had the propeller to the rear with the crew positioned at the front, but such aircraft had a much poorer performance. The British Vickers FB-5, which made its appearance in July 1915, was of this type but its top speed of 112kph (70mph) was not especially impressive.

DEFLECTOR GEAR

A French pilot, Roland Garros, came up with a solution to the tractor problem. In March 1915 he fitted steel plates to the propeller of a Morane-Saulnier L Parasol, a two-seater monoplane, so that bullets would be deflected away without causing damage. France's first dedicated fighter, the Morane-Saulnier N Scout, appeared shortly thereafter. This "deflector gear" gave the Allies an edge in the race to develop better fighters but this advantage was soon lost.

FOKKER E-TYPES

These German Army Air Service aircraft were designed by the Dutchman Antony Fokker and are regarded as the first true fighters. They saw action from mid-1915 and took a terrible toll of Anglo-French machines until spring 1916.

TYPE: E-III monoplane fighter
ENGINE: 100hp Oberursel
CREW: 1
CEILING: 3,650m (12,000ft)
TOP SPEED: 140kph (85mph)
ARMAMENT: 1 or 2 x 8mm (0.315in) machine-gun(s)

MAX IMMELMANN

Immelmann was one of the first *Experten* (or "aces") of the German Army Air Service. He shot down 15 Allied aircraft before his death in June 1916. He invented the Immelmann turn, an aerobatic manoeuvre still used by pilots. This is a combined backward loop and roll that can allow a fighter pilot who is being pursued to turn the tables on his pursuer.

Above: Max Immelmann, the "Eagle of Lille", one of the first fighter aces, who became a popular hero in Germany.

MORANE-SAULNIER TYPE N

This French fighter made its debut in late 1914 and was one of the first true fighters on the Western Front. Early models were fitted with deflector gear but later models carried the more advanced interrupter gear. It also saw service with Britain (as shown) and Russia.

ENGINE: 80/110hp Le Rhône
CREW: 1
CEILING: 4,000m (13,100ft)
TOP SPEED: 160kph (100mph)
ARMAMENT: 1 x 8mm (0.315in) machine-gun

VICKERS FB-5

This "pusher" fighter was the first ever British fighter and began arriving on the Western Front in mid-1915. It was soon outclassed by the Fokker E-types and production ended in early 1916 after some 100 aircraft had been built.

ENGINE: 100hp Gnome Monosoupape
CREW: 2
CEILING: 2,700m (8,800ft)
TOP SPEED: 112kph (70mph)
ARMAMENT: 1 x 0.303in (7.7mm) machine-gun

The Germans captured an example of the deflector gear in April 1915 and set about making a better version. Fokker, a Dutch company, came up with interrupter gear, a device that prevented a machine-gun from firing when a propeller blade passed immediately in front of its barrel. It was first tried out on the Fokker E-I monoplane and it had transformed air warfare by late 1915. Some 300 E-types, especially the single-seat E-III with a top speed of around 140kph (85mph), shot down more than a thousand Allied aircraft and took an especially heavy toll of the Vickers FB-5 in what was known as the "Fokker Scourge". The E-types were pre-eminent until the arrival of comparable Allied fighters in the spring of 1916.

AIR COMBAT TECHNIQUES

As fighters gradually appeared, leading pilots began to develop the tactics of air combat. Complex dogfighting was rare and victory usually went to the pilot who exploited the sun and clouds to sneak up behind his opponent and open fire at close range. Pilots recorded their successes, or "kills", and those who achieved more than five became recognized as "aces". Many were soon killed, however.

Right: Roland Garros (in beret) flew the first Allied aircraft to be fitted with deflector gear.

Balloons

Balloons played a number of vital roles in the war, such as protecting vulnerable sites from being attacked by aircraft, but their most important role was that of aerial observation despite the advent of reconnaissance aircraft.

Balloons, lighter-than-air, gas-filled envelopes lacking a metal or wooden frame, were widely used during World War I and were kept aloft by either hot air or a gas. They had two main roles – observation of the enemy on land or at sea, or as components in fixed anti-aircraft defence systems.

Artillery observation balloons were cheap to build and their wicker baskets offered a generally more stable viewing platform than an aircraft. They were tethered to the ground by wire(s) attached to a winch or winches and positioned behind friendly lines so that their crews could look for suitable targets or check the fall of artillery fire and correct it if necessary. They usually operated in groups of two or three to make the triangulation of a target more precise. Communication with the ground was initially by sema-phore flags or even by dropping weighted messages before the arrival of portable radio sets. These types of balloon were in service for much of the war, particularly up to 1917, but were

Above: The aircraft carrier HMS *Furious* with a Sea Scout Z anti-submarine balloon on its rear flight deck. *Furious* began life as a battle-cruiser but was successively updated for its new role.

increasingly replaced by better reconnaissance aircraft and aerial photography.

ATTACKING BALLOONS

The crews of observation balloons were vulnerable both to ground fire and attacks by fighters, and they were the only British airmen to be issued with parachutes as a matter of course

Left: British warships in Scapa Flow, the Grand Fleet's main base. A tethered balloon keeps watch for submarines or other hostile activity.

OBSERVATION BALLOONS

Such balloons were used to watch enemy activity behind the front line or to spot targets and correct the aim of the artillery. Conditions for the spotter were tolerable in good weather but abysmal in other circumstances.

Below: A British balloon is lowered to the ground at the end of a mission on the Western Front.

Above: A row of tethered balloons holding a wire barrage, designed to slice through the wings of any aircraft whose crew failed to spot the wires in time, pictured around north-east London.

as it took such a long time to winch them to the ground in an emergency. Yet pilots detested missions to destroy balloons as they involved flying behind enemy lines into areas usually heavily protected by anti-aircraft batteries and fighters.

Balloons were not easy to shoot down. Before the advent of incendiary or explosive bullets, standard rounds from a fighter's machine-gun would often pass harmlessly through the envelope. There was also a good chance that a fighter, which had to get very close to a balloon to make its machine-guns count, might become fatally entangled in, or have a wing sheared off by, the various steel wires that routinely dangled below the target. Destroying a balloon was such a feat of arms that all of the warring air forces designated it a "kill" in the same way as shooting down an enemy aircraft.

BALLOON BARRAGES

Balloons linked together with chains from which wires dangled to ensnare any attacking aircraft were also deployed to protect vulnerable airspace over valuable targets such as major cities and industrial sites. London was the most prominent case because of the frequent airship and heavy bomber raids it had to endure during the war. These tethered balloons were positioned to the north and east of the capital and were part of a defensive system that included fighter aircraft patrols, anti-aircraft batteries and searchlights.

Aside from their use in land operations, balloons were deployed in anti-submarine warfare, mostly by Britain's Royal Naval Air Service. They largely operated in the English Channel or Irish Sea and had the endurance and speed to act as lookouts for convoys. Several types were developed but the most common were the 70 designated Sea Scout Z (SSZ). These entered service in May 1915 and comprised a balloon from which the fuselage of a BE-2C biplane was suspended. The final development of the Sea Scout was termed the Coastal-class Airship, a design that could stay aloft for up to 24 hours and in which the BE-2C fuselage was replaced by a purpose-built gondola.

Zeppelins

German Zeppelins and other airship types carried out dozens of raids against Britain, France and Russia during the war but the British bore the brunt of their attacks, with 53 raids in total between 1914 and 1918.

In World War I rigid-frame airships were used most extensively by the German Army Air Service and the Imperial German Navy, in both reconnaissance or night-time bombing roles. Germany built two main types, the well-known Zeppelin and the little known Schütte-Lanz (SL). Both of these were kept aloft by highly pure but potentially explosive hydrogen, though they had different types of rigid frame.

AIRSHIP VARIANTS

The more common design was the Zeppelin, which was developed by Graf Zeppelin and was first accepted into German military service in March 1909. Zeppelins had a metal (duralumin) frame and came in a variety of designs. The early *L.3* was around 158.5m (520ft) long, was crewed by 16 men, and had a top speed of 72kph (45mph), while the more advanced

Above: German airships head out on a mission over England. The first attack came in January 1915 but the raids tailed off dramatically from 1917 onward.

R-type measured some 200m (650ft), had a crew of 19 and a top speed of 96kph (60mph).

The smaller Schütte-Lanz type was named after its designers, Professor Schütte and Doctor Lanz. SL airships had the drawback that their plywood frames tended to absorb atmospheric moisture too easily in flight. This made them difficult to control and they became unpopular with their crews.

The German Army put great store in its airships but its faith was shattered in the first weeks of the war. They were deployed

Left: French troops stand watch over the burnt-out remains, mostly twisted metal, of the German airship *L.39* on 6 April 1917.

on daylight reconnaissance missions over heavily defended areas of Belgium and France, and in August 1914 alone four were lost to ground fire and one was destroyed when a British fighter attacked it in its shed. The Army lost interest in airships from late 1916 and then abandoned them altogether in June 1917.

LONG-RANGE RAIDS

The German Navy, which had always led the way in airships, thereafter dominated operations and increasingly turned to night-time bombing. In total the German Naval Airship Division operated 73 airships during the war (59 Zeppelins, 8 Schütte-Lanz and 6 other types, such as the Parseval) and these made 342 bombing and 1,191 reconnaissance flights. Their main bombing targets were in England, especially London and other industrial areas, and Paris, although there were attempted raids on targets in Russia, including Baltic naval bases and the capital Petrograd (St Petersburg). Perhaps the most ambitious Zeppelin operation was that undertaken by *L.59* in late 1917. It was ordered to fly supplies from Bulgaria to German forces in East Africa. The mission (21–25 November) was aborted in mid-flight but *L.59* and its 22-man crew spent some 95 hours in the air and made a round trip of 6,750km (4,200 miles), braving violent storms and mechanical failures.

Zeppelins and SLs were in reality not as menacing as was believed. Their raids over England in particular did cause alarm but little damage and, in truth, they were very vulner-

able; 77 out of 115 Zeppelins were destroyed or damaged beyond repair, for example. Many crashed due to adverse weather – high winds and ice were especially dangerous – while others were shot down by ground fire or, increasingly, by high-altitude fighters. Sometimes bombs were dropped on airships from above, while some fighters like the French Nieuport 17 and the British Sopwith Camel were equipped with incendiary rockets, such as the French Le Prieur that appeared in 1916. Rockets were supplanted by incendiary bullets and their use was largely discontinued by 1918.

Accidents were also not uncommon. The worst came in January 1918 when five airships were destroyed in a fire at their base while they were undergoing maintenance.

THE LARGEST ZEPPELIN RAID

The biggest German airship raid on England took place on the night of 2 September 1916 and involved 11 Navy and 3 Army airships, most of them Zeppelins. A further two turned back early in the mission. The raiders struck up and down the East Coast, dropping 261 high-explosive and 202 incendiary bombs that did little damage but did kill 4 civilians and injure 12. One airship, *SL.11*, was shot down by a BE-2 fighter over Cuffley in Hertfordshire, just north of London.

Below: The spectacular end of a German airship. It was very rare for crew members to survive the downing of Zeppelins because of their combustibility.

Heavy Bombers

Heavy bombers made their debut during World War I. They were mostly deployed to undertake long-range strategic raids against military installation and industrial targets but they were also responsible for the deaths of many civilians.

Russia's Army Air Service had the most reliable heavy bomber at the outbreak of the war. It was based on Igor Sikorsky's civilian "Le Grand" from 1913, the world's first four-engined aircraft, and a military version, the Sikorsky IM (Ilya Mourometz), was ordered by the service in August 1914. It was a biplane design with an enclosed cabin, and a crew of six. It had a top speed of 96kph (60mph), a pair of machine-guns for defence and could carry some 535kg (1,180lb) of bombs. The IMs began operating against targets in eastern Poland in February 1915 and these

Below: The Russian-built Sikorsky IM (Ilya Mourometz) was one of the world's first successful heavy bombers and had a six-man crew.

raids were gradually extended to take in targets in Austria-Hungary and Germany. Some 400 sorties were launched by 73 bombers during 1914–17 and they proved highly successful and largely invulnerable. Only one was shot down, after itself destroying three of a group of attacking fighters, and just two others succumbed to various mechanical problems.

ITALIAN DESIGNS

Italy's fledgling air service, the Corpo Aeronautico Militare (CAM), was woefully prepared for war in 1915 but it did have a long-range bomber in the Caproni. CAM had focused on such aircraft because of the local conditions – the likely battle-field was mountainous, making tactical bombing in support of

GOTHA G-IV

The Gotha was the mainstay of Germany's heavy-bomber force during the war, and five variants were built in all. The most successful version, with 230 built, was the G-IV, which began operating in early 1917. Gothas were, however, fragile machines and clumsy to fly.

ENGINE: 3 x 260hp Mercedes DIV
CREW: 3
CEILING: 6,500m (21,325ft)
TOP SPEED: 140kph (87mph)
ARMAMENT: 3 x 7.92mm (0.312in) machine-guns, 500kg (1,100lb) bombs

ground operations problematic, but there were tempting long-range targets in both Austria-Hungary and the Balkans. Four types of Capronis (designated Ca2 to Ca5) were developed and around 750 were built in all. They came in several forms: some were biplanes while others were triplanes but they all had three engines. The Ca5 four-man biplane, introduced in early 1918, was ultimately the mainstay of the Italian strategic bombing force with a total of 280 being built.

THE GOTHA MENACE

The mainstay of the German Army Air Service's heavy bomber force was the Gotha G-series of twin-engined biplanes (designated G-I to G-V) that first entered service in 1915. These launched the first sustained strategic bombing offensive against London from bases around Ghent from June 1917. The most numerous type was the three-man G-IV which had a speed of around 140kph (87mph) and a range of 480km (300 miles). It was protected by three machine-guns and had a bomb load of some 500kg (1,100lb). The Germans also developed an even larger bomber, the Riesenflugzeug ("giant aircraft"), based on Sikorsky's IM type, that first entered full service in late 1916. Various companies built these advanced biplane bombers and

CAPRONI Ca5

The Caproni range of Italian heavy bombers made their debut during 1911 and launched their first bombing raid of World War I in August 1915. Four variants of the design were built and served with the Italian Army and Navy and the US Army Air Service.

ENGINE: 3 x 300hp Fiat
CREW: 2–4
CEILING: 4,550m (14,900ft)
TOP SPEED: 160km/h (100mph)
ARMAMENT: 2 x 6.5mm (0.256in) machine-guns, 910kg (2,000lb) bombs

there was no fully standardized design. The best was made by the Zeppelin-Staaken company. Its four-engined RVI first appeared in mid-1917. It had a seven-man crew, four machine-guns for defence, and carried up to 18 bombs.

BRITAIN'S REPLY

Britain's main heavy bombers were the twin-engined Handley Page O/100 (46 built) and O/400 (550 built). The former began operating in November 1916. Heavy O/100 losses during daylight raids led them to adopt night flying. The O/400 was a similar machine and went into full production in late 1917. It was expected to be the mainstay of the Independent Air Force's strategic bombing campaign against Germany in 1919, a role until then carried out by smaller bombers. Britain was also developing other heavy bombers, chiefly the four-engined Handley Page V/1500 and the twin-engined Vickers Vimy, but none saw action.

HANDLEY PAGE O/400

The HP O/400 entered service in the spring of 1918. A number were used in the bombing offensive against Germany. Although they carried a sizeable bomb load, they were also prone to accidents. Some 550 were built in Britain and a further 107 in the United States before the war's end.

ENGINE: 2 x 275hp Sunbeam or 2 x 375hp Rolls-Royce
CREW: 4
CEILING: 2,590m (8,500ft)
TOP SPEED: 160kph (100mph)
ARMAMENT: 3–5 x 0.303in (7.7mm) machine-guns, 820kg (1,800lb) bombs

Light Bombers

Largely developed to operate over or immediately beyond the battlefield to attack a wide variety of targets, light bombers later increasingly operated in direct support of attacks to destroy enemy positions that were holding up friendly forces.

Aircraft of this type gradually evolved during World War I as new designs with more powerful engines became available. Unlike the first under-powered aircraft that struggled to get a pilot off the ground, these could carry a practical if modest bomb load and were primarily used against targets in or near the front line. Some also flew longer-range missions but that was the exception rather than the norm. Most light bombers that saw service were two-seater, single-engined biplanes, although there were exceptions like the German AEG G-series that first appeared in 1916, which had three engines and a crew of three or four.

Although some countries, notably Britain and France, produced dedicated light bombers,

both they and other combatants used fighters or multi-purpose aircraft in the light-bomber role. There was some sense in this as fighters stood a better chance of survival if attacked, although they generally carried smaller bomb loads, while multi-purpose reconnaissance/light-bomber types could easily fulfil two roles. Light bombers often

Above: The British Airco DH-4 day bomber was both manoeuvrable and versatile and entered service from March 1917.

needed fighter escorts anyway as they were slower and less well armed.

The Royal Aircraft Factory's BE-2 of 1912 was one of the first British aircraft to fly bombing

VOISIN 3

France deployed the Voisin 3 pusher biplane, the only aircraft in any air force then to be fitted with a machine-gun as standard, from late 1914. Thanks to its steel airframe, it was a sturdy machine. It proved successful in short-range support missions but was also used as a strategic bomber, notably when 18 attacked two German poison-gas factories on 27 May 1915. Some were also sold to Russia.

ENGINE: 120hp Salmson 9M
CREW: 2
CEILING: 3,350m (11,000ft)
TOP SPEED: 105kph (65mph)
ARMAMENT: 100kg (220lb) bombs; 1 x 8mm (0.315in) machine-gun

missions but its two-man crew could only throw small bombs at a target and had only a rifle or pistol to defend themselves. Its replacement, the RE-7, arrived at the front from late 1915 and was soon found to be under-powered and under-armed, but it was at least given a machine-gun for protection and could carry 155kg (340lb) of bombs. Other British aircraft used in the light-bomber role included Airco's single-engined DH-4, which also saw considerable service with the American forces, and the company's less successful twin-engined DH-9.

FRENCH DESIGNS

The development of French light bombers followed a similar pattern. Voisin was perhaps the major manufacturer and its two-seater Voisin 3 was the first air-craft to carry a machine-gun when it began to appear in late 1914. Although its bomb load was limited to just 100kg (220lb), some 800 were built. New models were gradually introduced with better charac-teristics. The Voisin 8 entered

BE-2

The BE-2 was designed by Geoffrey de Havilland before the outbreak of the war and continued in service until 1916. One was the first British aircraft to land in France in 1914, while another was flown by the first officer to win a Victoria Cross in aerial warfare.

ENGINE: 70hp Renault
CREW: 2
CEILING: 3,000m (10,000ft)
TOP SPEED: 112kph (70mph)
ARMAMENT: hand-thrown bombs; sidearms or rifle

Below: The French Breguet Type XIV B2 light bomber entered service in the summer of 1917.

service in late 1916 and could carry some 80 per cent more bombs by weight but sacrificed so much speed and agility that heavy losses relegated it to night-time missions. The Voisin 10 of early 1918 had a better engine and nearly three times the bomb load of the Voisin 3. Other aircraft used in the light-bombing role were the success-ful multi-purpose Breguet B2 and B4, which saw service in 1915–18, and the Salmson 2, which appeared over the Western Front in early 1918.

GERMAN RESPONSES

Germany did not develop many light bombers, although the two-seater LVG C-II was deployed in this role during 1915–17. The German Army Air Service used fighters for light bombing but preferred to develop ground-attack or multi-purpose aircraft to undertake similar operations. LVG's C-V, for example, entered service in mid-1917 and performed recon-naissance, light-bombing and ground-attack missions success-fully until the Armistice.

Aces and Fighter Tactics

Although the truly great aces were undoubtedly expert pilots and skilled marksmen,
they had one particular trait that marked them out from all of their contemporaries
– their absolute ruthlessness when in air-to-air combat.

While it is true that the tactics of air combat developed significantly during the war, most aircraft were not shot down after prolonged bouts of air combat, and mass dogfights between dozens of fighters were virtually unknown until the later years of the conflict. The best way to down an opponent was to get behind and slightly below him at close range, preferably unseen in a faster, more manoeuvrable and better-armed aircraft. This last point cannot be overstressed as the air war in World War I was a technological struggle as much as anything else and the arrival of a better fighter frequently tipped the balance of power – at least until it was superseded by a better enemy aircraft.

Nevertheless, a handful of fighter pilots on all sides proved to be exceptionally skilled and were seen as aces. The French press invented the idea in 1915 to honour a pilot who had shot down five enemy aircraft and then the German Army Air Service required that a pilot score eight (later sixteen) kills before he could receive its highest decoration. The British authorities rather frowned on the idea of this type of personality cult, but set a benchmark in March 1918 announcing that a fighter pilot needed to score eight victories to win the Distinguished Flying Cross.

Above: US ace Edward "Eddie" Rickenbacker trained as a pilot in 1917, then joined and later led the elite 94th "Hat in the Ring" Squadron in 1918.

BILLY BISHOP

Canadian ace William "Billy" Bishop (1894–1956), seen here in front of his French-built Nieuport 17 Scout fighter, was one of the war's top-scoring pilots. He began flying fighters in March 1917 and scored his first victory on the 25th. He received a Victoria Cross in August for attacking a German aerodrome and destroying several enemy aircraft – all in a matter of just 37 minutes on 2 June. After the war, he rose to the rank of air marshal.

TOP ACES

As air combat was most intense over the Western Front, it was there where most aces were to be found. Leading the pack was Germany's Baron Manfred von Richthofen with 80 confirmed kills between August 1916 and April 1918. No one else in the German forces came close to his score but the second most successful German ace of the war, Ernst Udet, managed to down 62 aircraft. Three Allied aces came nearer to matching Richthofen – France's René Fonck with a score of 75, English pilot Edward "Mick" Mannock with 73, and Canadian William "Billy" Bishop with 72. Despite their prowess in air combat, aces

BARON MANFRED VON RICHTHOFEN

Richthofen (1892–1918) was a Prussian cavalry officer but transferred to the German Army Air Service in May 1915. He fought as an air observer on the Eastern Front, flew with bombers in Belgium and then undertook reconnaissance missions over Verdun. He thereafter began flying fighters and by April 1917 had shot down 52 aircraft, becoming a household name in the process. He commanded Jagdgeschwader 1 (Fighter Group 1), the renowned "Flying Circus", from June and his tally grew. He was killed by ground fire on 21 April 1918 with 80 kills to his credit.

Above: As Richthofen's fame grew he became a valuable propaganda tool for Germany but his loss was keenly felt.

ERNST UDET

Ernst Udet (1896–1941), seen here beside his Fokker D-VII fighter, was the highest-scoring German ace to survive the war, amassing 62 victories over the Western Front from the spring of 1918 onward. He was lucky, however, as in an early combat during 1917 he met the outstanding French ace Georges Guynemer. Udet's guns jammed as the fight began but Guynemer saw this and chivalrously flew off without attacking.

were far from invulnerable. Mannock was killed by ground fire and it is thought most likely that Richthofen suffered the same fate.

ELITE UNITS

Most of the rival air forces also contained fighter squadrons that could boast outstanding combat records and in some cases they also were the focus of intense propaganda campaigns to boost morale on the home front. The most famous of course was Manfred von Richthofen's "Flying Circus", which was a group of four 12-aircraft squadrons formed in late June 1917 that gained its name because of the aircraft's garish colour schemes.

The French also had their fighter elite, the *Cigognes* ("Storks"). This unit originally included just a single squadron but two more were added in

1915 and four more joined at a later date to form Combat Group XII. Most of France's leading aces served with the Storks including both Georges Guynemer (54 kills) and Fonck.

The United States also had an elite squadron but it actually took to the skies before the country entered the war in April 1917. The Lafayette Squadron was founded in 1916, when it was known as the American Squadron, and was staffed by American pilots already serving with the French as volunteers. Its 38 pilots scored 38 confirmed victories before they transferred to the United States Army Air Service in February 1918. The most successful US ace of the war did not actually serve with the squadron but ex-racing driver Eddie Rickenbacker shot down 26 aircraft and balloons in a brief career that began in March 1918.

Later Fighters

The latter part of the war saw the emergence of highly specialized fighters that flew higher and faster than ever before and their emergence meant the battle in the air swayed first one way and then the other in a hard-fought technological struggle.

The fighters of the second half of World War I were far superior to their predecessors. All combatant nations were now able to fit forward-firing machine-guns to their fighters and the later machines were also usually far more streamlined and fitted with more powerful engines. They therefore had a better rate of climb, greater speed, and were much more manoeuvrable. Better fighters

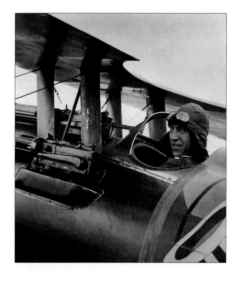

Above: US ace "Eddie" Rickenbacker pictured in his French-built Spad XIII fighter in June 1918.

The fighters of 1917–18 were mostly biplanes, although there were a few notable three-winged designs, chiefly the British Sopwith Triplane and the famed Fokker Dr-1 as flown for a time by Baron Manfred von Richthofen. The Fokker was introduced in June 1917 but was withdrawn in the autumn after a number of accidents. It briefly re-emerged in 1918 but was obsolescent by the summer.

appeared on both sides at regular intervals and thus air superiority would switch back and forth between the sides – often in just a few months – as new arrivals outclassed their older opponents.

BATTLES IN 1917

This was demonstrated in the Battle of Arras in the spring of 1917. The British enjoyed a 3:1 advantage in aircraft over the Germans but were reliant on the Royal Aircraft Factory's two-seater BE-2s and RE-8s. These were no match for the Albatros D-types and, during what became known to the British as "Bloody April", they lost 151 aircraft and 316 crew compared to German figures of 66 and 119. Yet the D-types were soon outclassed by British SE-5s and France's Spad S-VIIs.

FOKKER DR-1

This legendary German fighter entered service in the summer of 1917 as a stop-gap design and was not particularly successful – it was not especially fast, though it was very manoeuvrable. Nevertheless, some 329 were built before the war ended.

ENGINE: 110hp Oberursel or Le Rhône
CREW: 1
CEILING: 6,100m (20,000ft)
TOP SPEED: 165kph (102mph)
ARMAMENT: 2 x 7.92mm (0.312in) machine-guns

SOPWITH F-1 CAMEL

The Sopwith Camel was one of the best fighters of the war and was the first British aircraft to be built with two synchronized machine-guns. It was agile and had a good rate of climb but was difficult to fly. Many less experienced pilots paid the price.

ENGINE: Various including 130hp Clerget
CREW: 1
CEILING: 5,500m (18,000ft)
TOP SPEED: 185kph (115mph)
ARMAMENT: 2 x 0.303in (7.7mm) machine-guns

The Sopwith Triplane had a similarly short combat history. It made its debut on the Western Front in April 1917 with the Royal Naval Air Service (RNAS) and it simply outflew and outmanoeuvred any of its German rivals, so much so that some units amassed a large number of kills. The Canadian pilots of B Flight of the RNAS's No. 10 Squadron, commonly referred to as the Black Flight as its aircraft had their upper fuselages painted black, were a case in point. The flight consisted of just five Sopwith Triplanes yet these downed 87 German aircraft without loss between May and September 1917. However, their heyday was soon over as the Germans introduced better performing fighters and the last Sopwith Triplane was withdrawn from the Western Front during November.

BIPLANES

Triplanes were the exception and the single-seat biplane fighter fitted with two forward-firing machine-guns was the norm. All sides on the Western Front, where the most extensive air fighting took place, produced some outstanding designs. The French introduced their Spad S-XIII in the late summer of 1917, largely to replace the Spad S-VII, and it became the mainstay of the country's fighter strength as well as equipping Belgian, Italian and US squadrons. The British Sopwith Scout, which was nicknamed "Pup", appeared in numbers in late 1916 and was highly manoeuvrable, if underpowered and lightly armed. The Pup was superseded by the Sopwith F-1 Camel from July

FOKKER D-VIII

The Fokker D-VIII was one of the last German fighters to enter service on the Western Front and was basically a high-winged monoplane version of the previous D-VII biplane. It won a competition to find a new-generation fighter in April 1918 but it was soon plagued with problems – three of the first six to be delivered suffered catastrophic wing collapses. The problem was traced to some inflexible wing spars and these were replaced. The D-VIII was an extremely fast aircraft but, because of its early design flaws, only 85 ever reached the front.

Left: The Fokker D-VIII had a top speed of 200kph (124mph) and had two forward firing machine-guns but saw limited service.

1917 and it became Britain's leading fighter for the remainder of the war, shooting down some 1,300 enemy aircraft. Also in service in large numbers was the effective SE-5.

Germany's last notable biplane fighter was the Fokker D-VII, which was actually built by both Fokker and Albatros. It first saw action in May 1918 but despite its manoeuvrability, especially at high altitudes, the Allies would keep almost total air superiority due to some good aircraft but more importantly thanks to superior numbers.

Below: Australian troops with a captured Albatros D-III fighter, one of the most successful German fighters of the latter part of the war.

NAVAL WEAPONS

Operations at sea during World War I were dominated by battleships and naval strategy, developing into a naval arms race between Britain and Germany. This chapter looks at the different types of warships and submarines, from the early surface raiders and pre-dreadnought battleship to U-boats and battle-cruisers.

Image: An armed German military submarine comes to the surface.

Surface Raiders

The Imperial German Navy intended to launch a variety of surface ships against Britain's maritime trade routes which stretched across the globe but most of the raiders were sunk, lost or interned during the first months of the war.

Crippling an opponent by destroying his maritime trade and merchant fleet was a well-established naval strategy by 1914. As submarines were still an unknown quantity and as those available did not have the range to operate globally, many navies earmarked other vessels to undertake such duties. These were either purpose-built or converted civilian craft and the three main types were generally known as commerce raiders, armed merchant cruisers and auxiliary commerce raiders. They mostly operated far from home and relied on colonies, specially designated freighters or neutral ports for resupply.

COMMERCE RAIDERS

Germany had eight commerce raiders. Seven of these were with the East Asiatic Squadron in the Pacific and one, *Karlsruhe*, was in the West Indies. Four of the Pacific raiders were sunk at the Battle of the Falkland Islands in December 1914 while a fifth, *Dresden*, was scuttled in March 1915. The squadron's

remaining pair had equally brief careers. *Emden* successfully cruised the south-west Pacific and Indian Ocean between August and early November 1914 but then succumbed to the Australian cruiser *Sydney*.

The squadron's final cruiser, *Königsberg*, headed into the western Indian Ocean intending to sink Allied ships using the Suez Canal. It sank just two ships before the British found its hiding place in the River Rufiji's delta in German East Africa (now in Tanzania). An old ship was scuttled across the river's mouth to prevent any

escape and the raider was eventually damaged by fire from two British monitors and then scuttled on 11 July 1915.

The cruiser stationed in the West Indies, *Karlsruhe*, sank three vessels in the mid-Atlantic shortly after the outbreak of war and then sailed into the South Atlantic where it netted some 14 freighters between 31 August and 14 October 1914. *Karlsruhe* then headed into the Caribbean, with the intention of hunting through the Bahamas but succumbed to an unexplained internal explosion while at anchor on 4 November.

Right: *Seeadler*, a German merchant raider, made one successful cruise beginning in December 1916 and captured 15 Allied merchant ships in the Atlantic and Pacific in 225 days.

Seeadler was a three-masted windjammer built in Scotland as the *Pass of Balmaha*.

The ship was wrecked on a reef in the South Pacific and the crew eventually interned in Chile.

The interior was modified with the addition of facilities for prisoners, better crew quarters and hidden gun positions.

The hull was built in steel by the Robert Duncan Company, Port Glasgow.

SMS *SEEADLER*

TYPE: Converted sailing ship
LAID DOWN: 1888
DISPLACEMENT: 1,571 tons
CREW: Not known
SPEED: Variable
MAIN ARMAMENT: 2 x 10.5cm (4.1in) guns

ARMED MERCHANT CRUISERS

Armed merchant cruisers (AMCs) were usually fast passenger liners converted for military use by being fitted with armaments. They were used by Britain, France and Germany. The British had the greatest number and their 10th Cruiser Squadron consisted of 20 AMCs that protected the sea lanes between Britain and Iceland until 1917. The Allied AMCs proved to be vulnerable both to mines and torpedoes, and losses were unacceptably high – the British lost 12 and the French 13. The survivors were mostly converted to troop transports and hospital ships from 1916.

Germany used its AMCs exclusively in the aggressive role of commerce raiding but they were largely unsuccessful. Some had brief but spectacular careers, like the fast liner *Kaiser Wilhelm der Grosse*, which sank several ships before 26 August 1914 when it was scuttled by its crew after it had been disabled by the British cruiser *Highflyer* off Spanish Morocco. A second, *Cap Trafalgar*, was sunk by a British AMC, *Carmania*, in the South Atlantic on 14 August 1914. Two others, *Prinz Eitel Friedrich* and *Kronprinz Wilhelm*, were interned by the US authorities in March and April 1915, respectively.

ARMED COMMERCE RAIDERS

Auxiliary commerce raiders were essentially civilian craft fitted with hidden weapons. Germany's were often auxiliary minelayers converted to look like Scandinavian freighters, usually sailing under a neutral flag. Around ten saw service in the war and some were highly successful.

Möwe is considered the most renowned. It sank 34 merchant ships in two sorties and one of its mines sank the British pre-dreadnought battleship *King Edward VII* in January 1916.

Below: HMS *King Edward VII* sinking after hitting *Möwe's* mine.

SMS *EMDEN*

Emden's career was brief but spectacular. During August – November 1914 it sank 18 British merchant ships, captured 5 and sank a Russian cruiser and a French destroyer. *Emden* is shown below wrecked on Direction Island after being tracked down by Allied ships.

TYPE: Light cruiser
LAID DOWN: 1908
DISPLACEMENT: 3,650 tons
CREW: 321
SPEED: 24.5 knots
MAIN ARMAMENT: 10 x 10.5cm (4.1in) guns

SMS *KÖNIGSBERG*

Königsberg undertook operations off the coast of East Africa, sinking just two ships, including *Pegasus*, an old British cruiser. *Königsberg* took refuge in an East African river delta and was tracked down and sunk in 1915.

TYPE: Light cruiser
LAID DOWN: 1907
DISPLACEMENT: 3,400 tons
CREW: 350
SPEED: 23.5 knots
MAIN ARMAMENT: 10 x 10.5cm (4.1in) guns

Anti-submarine Barriers

Britain struggled to fight German U-boats in the early days of the war. Barriers of steel-net mesh were moored to the seabed in the hope of entangling the U-boats, while mines and fast warships were used to blow up the boats.

No ship-mounted weapons were capable of sinking submerged submarines when war broke out in August 1914. The British, who had the most to fear from submarines, soon began building maritime net barriers, commonly referred to as barrages. These either forced submarines to the surface, where they could be tackled by naval gunfire or rammed by warships, or left them at the mercy of tethered mines positioned with the nets. Perhaps the most successful barrages were those developed to prevent German U-boats from reaching their hunting grounds in the eastern Atlantic by way of the English Channel or through the North Sea. All U-boats had to pass

Below: A German U-boat at sea. This is the *U-9* which sank three elderly British cruisers off the Dutch coast on 22 September 1914.

Above: A mine of the type used in the Allied North Sea barrage built during 1918.

through these areas on their journeys between their patrol areas and their home bases in occupied Belgium and in Germany itself.

BLOCKING THE CHANNEL
The British first built a barrage between Dover and the Belgian coast to prevent attacks on their troopships crossing to France in August 1914. This initial effort was deemed inadequate and a 25km (15.5 mile) barrage stretching between Dover and Ostend was begun the following February. The line comprised indicator nets – lengths of steel mesh up to 100m (110yds) long that were positioned by drifters, set at various depths and moored to the seabed. Any U-boat that became entangled in one would either have to surface or drag the netting and its easily identifiable surface buoys away with it. The drifters were in radio contact with fast warships that could then be directed to the target and tackle the submarine with gunfire or by ramming when it had to surface for air.

Right: A British depth charge explodes during a hunt for a U-boat. Aggressive countermeasures would ultimately prove superior to the passive anti-submarine barriers.

The system, which gradually became more and more extensive and began to incorporate mines, was far from foolproof. The early contact mines were unreliable, while U-boat captains were often able to avoid the nets by travelling on the surface at night. The Dover Barrage did have its successes. U-boats were briefly prohibited from passing through the Channel for 12 months after April 1915, while better mines, more frequent night patrols and searchlights all played their part in improving the barrage. At least 12 submarines were lost in the barrage and the U-boats finally ceased using the Channel route in August 1918.

The route into the North Atlantic by way of the North Sea was not tackled until mid-July 1917. The building of a huge barrage between the Orkneys and the Norwegian coast was largely the brainchild of an American naval officer, Admiral Henry Mayo. He successfully argued that his country's new magnetic mine, which exploded when a submarine entered its magnetic field rather than needing direct contact, was appropriate for the task. The mine-laying took place during June–October 1918 and it was largely undertaken by US

Right: An aerial photograph of the anti-submarine barrage at Scapa Flow in the Orkneys, the Royal Navy's most important base and home of the bulk of the Grand Fleet.

crews, who laid more than 80 per cent of the 69,000 mines deployed. Yet for all that effort only three U-boats were confirmed sunk in the minefields.

OTRANTO BARRAGE
The third great Allied barrage was built in the Mediterranean as a way of preventing Austro-Hungarian and German surface warships and submarines from entering the sea from their bases in the northern and eastern Adriatic. It stretched across the Strait of Otranto from the heel of Italy to Valona (Vlorë) in Albania. Construction of the barrage began in late 1915 but the 100km (60 miles) of anti-submarine nets patrolled by numbers of warships were never wholly secure and only one U-boat was destroyed.

Battle-cruisers

Inspired by Admiral Fisher, the Royal Navy developed battle-cruisers in what proved to be a rather flawed attempt to create a new class of warship that was armed like a dreadnought battleship but had the greater speed of a cruiser.

Although cruisers were a long-established type of warship by the outbreak of World War I, the larger battle-cruisers were a relatively new concept and had not been tested in action. The idea came from the fertile brain of Britain's Admiral John Fisher, who was also responsible for the powerful dreadnought type of battleship. Fisher wanted a class of warships that could act independently, or form the nucleus of a detached squadron, or work in conjunction with the main battlefleet of dreadnoughts. In this last mission, battle-cruisers were to act in the scouting and reconnaissance role, seeking out the enemy's main fleet and reporting back on its position. Their heavy armament, which was comparable to that of a dreadnought, meant that they could destroy smaller warships, while their high speed meant they could outrun bigger opponents. Battle-cruisers were originally known as fast armoured cruisers but took on their more common name in 1912.

Below: A close-up of one of the turrets of the British battle-cruiser *Tiger* – an early attempt to provide the warship with a means of aerial reconnaissance and firepower.

FIRST BATTLE-CRUISERS

Britain launched its first three battle-cruisers, HMS *Invincible*, *Indomitable* and *Inflexible*, during 1909. These, and a second group of three, carried eight 12in (305mm) guns (dreadnoughts mostly had ten) and displaced 17,250 tons. Later classes carried larger guns. *Renown* and *Repulse*, launched in 1916, each had six 15in (380mm) guns. The Royal Navy had most battle-cruisers with 12 built in 1908–17. Only Germany and Japan copied the design and had them available in 1914.

Battle-cruisers did have successes. *Invincible* and *Inflexible* sank two less-powerful German armoured cruisers during the Battle of the Falklands in late 1914, while on detached service from the main battlefleet. Germany's own battle-cruisers also enjoyed some successes while acting independently, not least when they severely dented the British public's faith in the Royal Navy by bombarding a number of towns on Britain's east coast. Yet these victories

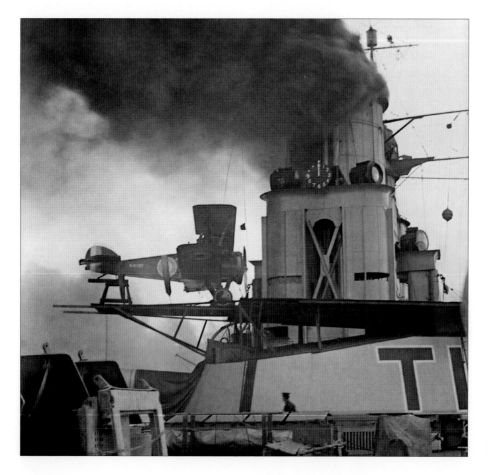

HMS *TIGER*	
CLASS:	Only ship of its type
LAID DOWN:	1912
DISPLACEMENT:	28,500 tons
CREW:	1,185
SPEED:	30 knots
MAIN ARMAMENT:	8 x 13.5in (343mm) guns

masked some serious technical and design shortcomings, especially in Britain's battle-cruisers, that were only fully exposed in larger fleet actions.

Part of the problem was that their name was perhaps misinterpreted by some officers and led them to believe mistakenly that battle-cruisers could take their place in the main line of battle. Their armament suggested they could take on similarly armed battle-cruisers or dreadnoughts but their armour, which had been reduced to give them their higher speed, actually meant that they could not stand punishment from the heavy guns carried by either.

SMS *DERFFLINGER*

SMS *Derfflinger* was completed in mid-1914 and took part in raids along the east coast of England and the Battle of the Dogger Bank in early 1915 before being badly damaged during the Battle of Jutland in 1916.

SISTER SHIPS: *Hindenburg, Lützow*
LAID DOWN: 1912
DISPLACEMENT: 28,000 tons
CREW: 1,112
SPEED: 28 knots
MAIN ARMAMENT: 8 x 30.5cm (12in) guns

SMS *GOEBEN*

Goeben was handed over to the Turkish Navy in August 1914, although still German-crewed. It operated in the Black Sea against Russia and later in the Mediterranean. Damaged by mines in January 1918, it spent the rest of the war in dry dock.

SISTER SHIP: *Moltke*
LAID DOWN: 1909
DISPLACEMENT: 22,640 tons
CREW: 1,053
SPEED: 29 knots
MAIN ARMAMENT: 10 x 28cm (11in) guns

PROBLEMS IN ACTION

The Battle of Jutland in May 1916 revealed the truth. Three British battle-cruisers, *Invincible*, *Indefatigable* and *Queen Mary*, were sent to the bottom in quick time, blown apart in an instant by single salvoes of shells. The shells easily penetrated their overly thin armour and then exploded causing a fire that detonated ammunition that was being stored incorrectly. Germany's own battle-cruiser squadron did not escape without loss or damage either. The *Lützow* was sunk and all of the other ships were hit repeatedly, not least the *Seydlitz*, yet all reached their home port. Their survival was partly due to luck, but also to good seamanship and design precautions to prevent secondary internal explosions during the heat of battle. Neither Britain nor Germany lost any more battle-cruisers during World War I. Their vulnerability was clear to all but the growth of naval aviation gradually removed the need for them to act in the reconnaissance role for the main battlefleet.

SMS *SEYDLITZ*

CLASS: Only ship of its type
LAID DOWN: 1911
DISPLACEMENT: 25,000 tons
CREW: 1,068
SPEED: 30 knots
MAIN ARMAMENT: 10 x 28cm (11in) guns

Pre-dreadnought Battleships

Although they no longer had the speed and gunpower to lead a battlefleet into a full-scale action, ageing pre-dreadnought types were still able to perform many vital roles to play in the battle for naval supremacy.

When the Royal Navy's HMS *Dreadnought* was launched in 1906, its gunpower made every other battleship in existence obsolete and sparked a worldwide naval arms race. Yet no navy was going to scrap its very costly pre-dreadnought battleships. Consequently many outdated pre-dreadnoughts remained in use when war broke out in 1914.

NUMBERS IN SERVICE

On the Allied side, the Royal Navy had 29 operational pre-dreadnoughts with 20 in mothballs, the French had 17 largely based in the Mediterranean, Italy 8 and Russia 9. Two countries that subsequently joined the Allied cause, Japan and the USA, had 23 and 16 respectively. The fleets of the Central Powers also contained pre-dreadnoughts – Germany had more than 20, Austria-Hungary 12 and Turkey 2.

The pre-dreadnoughts came in a variety of designs and were of varying ages. The Royal Navy and Germany, for example, had such ships that had been built between 1892 and 1908 and, while they differed in detail, they did have some similarities. They typically displaced 10,000–14,000 tons, with the more recent ships being larger. They usually carried four main guns of 28cm (11in) calibre (Germany) and 12in (30.5cm) (Britain) and had secondary armaments of 10–14 lighter guns. Although the pre-dreadnoughts' firepower seemed impressive, they were wholly outclassed by the dreadnoughts, and most naval strategists agreed that the former would take a terrible pounding from the latter in a full-blown fleet action.

AT WAR

The German Navy needed all the large warships it could muster to oppose the British in

Below: The French *Suffren* dated back to 1899 but was torpedoed and sunk by *U-52* off Lisbon in 1916 after service in the Dardanelles.

Main bridge, not covered or protected in any way from either the weather or enemy fire

Gunnery control position. Raised as high as possible for best visibility

Rear twin 12in gun turret (under a protective awning in this harbour photo)

HMS *Formidable*

Forward twin 12in gun turret

Boom for supporting anti-torpedo netting, sometimes used when at anchor

Smoke from coal-fired engines. Many dreadnoughts used more modern oil-fired machinery

Side-mounted 6in secondary gun position

HMS *FORMIDABLE*

FORMIDABLE CLASS
TYPE: Pre-dreadnought battleship
LAID DOWN: 1898
DISPLACEMENT: 15,000 tons
CREW: 780
SPEED: 18.5 knots
ARMAMENT: 4 x 12in (305mm) + 12 x 6in (152mm) guns

the North Sea so its High Seas Fleet retained some of its pre-dreadnoughts. The gamble paid off, because the fleets only met once and only one German pre-dreadnought was lost to enemy fire – SMS *Pommern* at Jutland in 1916. Other German pre-

Right: The pre-dreadnought *Pommern* was one of six German pre-dreadnoughts at the Battle of Jutland in 1916. *Pommern* was sunk with all hands by a torpedo from the British destroyer *Faulknor*.

dreadnoughts did give valuable service in the Baltic but largely in support of ground operations.

The Royal Navy adopted a slightly different plan. Its pre-dreadnoughts were quickly removed from the main Grand Fleet but many were sent on subsidiary missions like shore bombardments, or to theatres where they were unlikely to meet more powerful enemy

dreadnoughts. Most ended up in the Mediterranean operating against Turkey.

In all, Britain lost 11 pre-dreadnoughts in the war. France and Russia each lost 4, Italy 2 and Japan 1. The Central Powers also had losses but not on the same scale. Aside from Germany's *Pommern*, the Turkish Navy had two sunk and Austria-Hungary one.

Seaplanes and Flying Boats

*Amphibious aircraft were an unknown quantity at the outbreak of war but they
proved invaluable as they performed several roles including those of reconnaissance
and bombing from both coastal bases and warships themselves.*

Seaplanes, aircraft fitted with floats so that they can take off and land on water, and flying boats, aircraft with waterproof hulls that can perform similarly, were used by most nations in World War I. Their main role was maritime reconnaissance but they also engaged in air-to-air combat, made anti-shipping sorties and raided coastal installations. Most seaplanes operated from coastal air stations but some, British examples in particular, operated from ships known as seaplane tenders.

However the aircraft were launched and recovered, maritime aviation was still in its infancy and the available aircraft could only be used in calm conditions. Bombs were the

Below: A pre-war seaplane built by the German company Albatros. Their main contribution to naval aviation during the conflict was the W-4 single-seat fighter.

main anti-ship weapon. Britain and Germany experimented with torpedoes but found that they were usually too heavy for existing engines to cope with.

IN BRITISH SERVICE

British seaplanes were operated by the Royal Naval Air Service (RNAS), the largest maritime air

force of the conflict, which came into being on 1 January 1914. It eventually had some 50 squadrons that operated from a similar number of coastal stations. The RNAS deployed a

Below: A German Friedrichshafen floatplane. The company produced floatplanes during World War I.

variety of seaplanes. The twin-engined Norman Thompson NT-4 and NT-4A equipped several squadrons and carried light bombs for anti-submarine work. One of the most successful later designs was the Felixstowe F-type flying boat, which began operating from 1917. Although slow at 150kph (95mph), these four-man aircraft handled well and could stay aloft for up to 10 hours. An F-type shot down the German airship *L.62* in May 1918 and

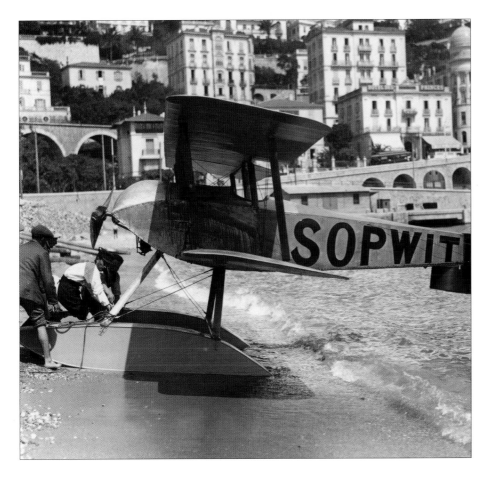

Above: A pre-war version of the British Sopwith Tabloid of the type that, with some modification, served as a naval reconnaissance and light bomber aircraft during the war.

five F-2As with a Curtiss H-12 took part in one of the very few battles between seaplanes. On 4 June 1918, they saw off 14 German aircraft after a dogfight, destroying 6 for the loss of just the Curtiss.

The first successful launch of an aerial torpedo was in July 1914 from a British aircraft and the world's first torpedo-bomber was the two-seat Short 184, which entered service with the RNAS in 1915. A 184 flying off Gallipoli from the seaplane tender *Ben-My-Chree* in August 1915 became the first aircraft to sink a ship with a torpedo. Despite this success, using torpedoes remained dangerous for the dropping aircraft and in the case of the Short 184 and the later 320 their use was discontinued. Other major British seaplanes were Sopwith's Schneider (1915) and Baby (1916).

GERMAN DESIGNS

Germany developed its own naval aviation service. It largely relied on a handful of manufacturers, such as Friedrichshafen, which produced the FF-33 series from late 1914. The main reconnaissance model, the FF-33e, was fitted with a two-way radio and carried a load of hand-thrown bombs, while the FF-33l was the seaplane fighter version. These types were superseded by the FF-49 from May 1917, a more robust aircraft that was better suited to the harsh conditions likely to be encountered in the North Sea. Other types included the Albatros W-4 floatplane fighter

and the Hansa-Brandenburg series – the CC, KDW, W-12 and W-29.

Both Austria-Hungary and Italy deployed maritime aviation units. The former relied on German types, like the Hansa-Brandenburg CC, but did also produce the two-seat Löhner L flying boat, one of which sank the French submarine *Foucault* on 15 September 1916. The Italians produced several such aircraft including the Macchi M-5 biplane fighter.

German Submarines

The Imperial German Navy began the war with very few submarines but they started to grow in importance and eventually became the main weapon in the campaign to bring Britain to its knees by strangling its maritime trade routes.

Germany deployed the most technically advanced and largest fleet of submarines of all during World War I but actually had none in service before 1906. Its navy had around 30 submarines available in August 1914 but by the end of the war a further 350 or so had seen active service. Their operational peak came in June 1917 when 61 were at sea.

The Imperial German Navy actually produced very few different types of boat during the war as its planners rightly believed that concentrating on fewer types made production, maintenance and the training of crews much more straightforward. Larger boats designed for long-range operations were given U- numbers, and there were smaller, short-range UB- and UC-boats that usually operated in shallower coastal waters.

Above: Crewmen watch over the engine room machinery in a U-boat. The image gives a good idea of the cramped working conditions aboard a World War I submarine.

Below: A UB-III class U-boat slices through rough seas off the German island of Heligoland in the southeastern North Sea.

U-BOAT TYPES

The term U-boat derives from *Unterseeboot* ("submarine boat") and these spearheaded the operations against British maritime commerce. They were built in batches and each differed in some way but overall became larger and more powerful as the war progressed. The

UC-1

UC-1 (illustrated) was Germany's original mine-laying submarine, the first of a class of 15, and appeared in 1915. It carried 12 mines which were deployed downwards through hatches in the keel. Surface armament was one machine-gun. It was 55m (180ft) long and had a surface speed of 6.5 knots (5 knots submerged). The *UC-1*'s chief weakness was its endurance, a mere 1,280km (800 miles) at 5 knots. It had a 16-man crew. The boat was lost on 19 July 1917 off Nieuport, Belgium, somewhat ironically probably to a mine.

650-ton *U-21* launched in 1913 had a surface speed of around 15 knots and some 9 knots submerged. It had a crew of 35 and carried four torpedo tubes and an 8.6cm (3.4in) deck gun. *U-140*, launched in late 1917, was much bigger. It displaced 1,930 tons and could cruise on the surface at nearly 16 knots or submerged at close to 8 knots. It had a crew of 64 and its weapons comprised six tubes and two 15cm (5.9in) deck guns. Its range was also more than three times that of *U-21*.

CARGO U-BOATS

The biggest of the U-boats were the Deutschland class, which appeared in 1916 and started out as unarmed cargo-carrying vessels. *Deutschland* itself caused something of a stir when it sailed as a merchant ship from Kiel to Baltimore in the then-neutral USA, partly to return with war materials but also as a propaganda mission. It arrived at its destination on 9 July and returned home with a cargo of various key metals. The seven vessels, *U-151* to *U-157*, were later converted into fighting submarines. They had two

tubes and a 15cm (5.9in) deck gun. Two of them were sunk but *U-155* proved to be very successful, sinking a total of 19

UB-1

This small submarine was the lead boat in a class of eight. They were all transported in sections to either Belgium or the Adriatic Sea where they operated for the duration. *UB-1* itself was wrecked in the Adriatic Sea and scrapped.

TYPE: Coastal submarine
LAID DOWN: 1914
DISPLACEMENT: 127 tons
CREW: 14
SPEED: 6.5 knots (surfaced)
MAIN ARMAMENT: 2 x 45.7cm (18in) torpedo tubes

Allied vessels on its first sortie to the Azores area in June–September 1917.

UB-boats became operational from spring 1915. The earliest batches, *UB-1* to *UB-17*, were found to be unsuitable for even the most basic anti-shipping role and were superseded by the larger UB-II class boats, *UB-18* to *UB-47*. These were faster, 9 knots rather than 6, and had a much greater range. The boats were first commissioned in 1915. The next UB-III class (*UB-48* to *UB-136*) did not emerge until the last year of the war. These were larger still, roughly four times the displacement of the first batch, with five torpedo tubes and one deck gun.

UC-boats were similarly conceived for short-range tasks but operated as minelayers. These first appeared in the English Channel in mid-1915 and also served in the Baltic, Black and Mediterranean Seas. Larger UC-II boats, numbers *UC-16* to *UC-79*, began operating in 1916 and they carried 18 rather than 12 mines and had an impressive range. A third batch, the UC-III class, was ordered in 1917 but did not see action.

Seaplane Tenders and Aircraft Carriers

Naval aviation was very much in its infancy at the outbreak of the war in 1914 but over the following years the British in particular began to experiment with a variety of warships capable of carrying aircraft into battle.

Attempts to deploy aircraft from warships in World War I were largely advanced by Britain's Royal Naval Air Service. Its first seaplane tender was an old converted cruiser, *Hermes*, sunk by a torpedo in October 1914, but the first true aircraft carrier was *Ark Royal*, an ex-collier that entered service in December 1914. The Royal Navy also transformed several cross-Channel ferries into lightly armed seaplane tenders from 1914 onwards. The ferries' relatively high speed was important because it allowed them to maintain pace with the more conventional warships of the main battlefleet.

FIRST BATTLES

Three, *Engadine*, *Empress* and *Riviera*, were converted that autumn and, while they could in theory at least fly wheeled aircraft from their decks, they invariably winched seaplanes

HMS *FURIOUS*

The forward flight deck on the ex-battle-cruiser HMS *Furious* allowed aircraft to take off but they could not land at sea. As first converted, *Furious* could carry 3 Short 184 seaplanes and 5 Sopwith Pup fighters.

DISPLACEMENT: 22,000 tons
CREW: 737
SPEED: 32.5 knots
MAIN ARMAMENT: 10 x 4in (101.6mm) guns

fitted with floats into and out of the water. Nevertheless, they proved their worth by making the first-ever naval aviation raid when they launched seven aircraft against the Zeppelin sheds near Cuxhaven on 25 December 1914. *Engadine* later served in the North Sea and was present at the Battle of Jutland in 1916.

The three other conversions were the larger *Ben-My-Chree*, *Manxman* and *Videx*. A milestone in naval aviation was achieved by the last in November 1915 when a Bristol Scout C aircraft became the first-ever land-based aircraft to achieve take-off at sea. *Ben-My-Chree* went to the Dardanelles in the summer of 1915 and one of its Short 184 seaplanes made the first successful aerial torpedo attack that August. There was a final group of seaplane tenders that entered service in 1915–17, including the ex-liners *Campania*, *Nairana*

Below: A fast cross-Channel ferry was converted into the seaplane tender HMS *Engadine* in 1914 and took part in a raid on the German airship base at Cuxhaven on 25 December.

Armament consisted of 2 x 4in (101.6mm) guns and a single 6pdr (57mm) anti-aircraft gun

The ship had a length of 94.5m (310ft) and a beam of 12.1m (40ft)

The hangar could house up to three aircraft

Engadine displaced 1,676 tons

Right: HMS *Argus* was the first flush-deck carrier from which aircraft could take off and land but did not enter service until October 1918.

and *Pegasus*, although their performance was generally no better or worse than their predecessors'. *Campania* saw little service before being lost in a storm in late 1918, while *Nairana* and *Pegasus* served in the North Sea before sailing for the Mediterranean during the same year.

France and Russia also developed tenders. The former began by converting a torpedo-boat depot ship, *Foudre*, so that by 1913 it had sufficient hangar space to carry a number of seaplanes. The French built just four more. The ex-passenger liner *Campinas* was converted in 1915 and again served in the eastern Mediterranean. Three cross-Channel ferries were also converted – *Rouen* acted as a convoy escort in the Mediterranean, while *Nord* and *Pas-de-Calais* operated in the

Channel. Russia deployed six seaplane tenders with its Black Sea Fleet.

AIRCRAFT CARRIERS
The use of wheeled aircraft on tenders and carriers was advanced by the arrival in 1916 of more powerful aircraft, notably Sopwith's Strutter and Pup, that could take off from short decks. However, they could not be landed and pilots had to ditch into the sea after a mission. The British tried to resolve this problem by further modifying *Furious*, a former

light battle-cruiser, in late 1917. By March 1918 it had two flight decks and extensive hangar space but turbulence from the central superstructure still made landing at sea very hazardous. Conversion work on the first true flush-deck aircraft carrier, the former liner *Argus*, had begun in late 1916 but both it and the first purpose-built carrier, *Hermes*, did not see action before the war's end.

HMS *CAMPANIA*

The ex-liner *Campania* entered service as an aircraft carrier in May 1915. It could carry ten seaplanes but the sloping forward flight deck was too short for aircraft to take off safely.

LAID DOWN: 1893
DISPLACEMENT: 18,000 tons
CREW: 600
SPEED: 22 knots
MAIN ARMAMENT: 6 x 4.7in (119mm) guns

THE TONDERN RAID

This British attack against a Zeppelin base on the German–Dutch border on 18 July 1918 was the only occasion in the war when aircraft were launched from an aircraft carrier. Seven Sopwith Camels carrying bombs flew off the deck of *Furious* at dawn; six attacked the target and two airships, *L.54* and *L.60*, were destroyed. Two aircraft made it to neutral Denmark, while three others ditched in the sea. The fate of the sixth aircraft remains unknown but five pilots and one aircraft survived from the attacking force.

Dreadnoughts

HMS Dreadnought, *the first modern battleship, was such a revolutionary design when it was launched that it instantly made all previous battleships obsolete and sparked a dangerous naval arms race between Britain and Germany.*

At the outbreak of the war naval commanders believed that the war at sea would be decided by a single titanic clash between surface fleets. This view was especially prevalent among the officers of Britain's Grand Fleet and Germany's High Seas Fleet, two powerful forces of warships that fully expected to clash somewhere in the North Sea. This view was based on key moments in naval history – most recently when the Imperial Japanese Navy had crushed Russia's Baltic Fleet during the Battle of Tsushima in 1905.

Naval engagements had usually been decided by the largest warships of both sides – battleships – taking each other on, and no one believed that World War I naval battles would be any

Above: HMS *Dreadnought* is launched in 1906. It served throughout the war, only being decommissioned in 1919.

Below: HMS *Dreadnought*. It sank one warship during the conflict, *U-29* in 1915.

different. Up to the early 1900s all navies had battleships that were generally similar in design but that all changed when HMS *Dreadnought* appeared. This revolutionary British warship was built in a never-matched 14 months and completed in December 1906. The driving force behind the project was the country's First Sea Lord, Admiral John Fisher, arguably the most dynamic and far-sighted naval officer of his generation. *Dreadnought* was a quantum leap in warship design. It quite simply made every other existing battleship outdated at a stroke.

GUNS AND TURBINES

Dreadnought was the first "all big gun" warship and it mounted ten powerful 12in (305mm) guns. By comparison the Royal Navy's latest pre-dreadnought battleships carried just four

The battleship had a displacement of 17,900 tons and was 160.3m (526ft) long

Its main armament consisted of 10 x 12in (305mm) guns, two of them in this forward turret

Steam turbines gave a top speed of 22 knots

Right: Evidence of the growing
naval arms race. German Nassau-
class dreadnoughts on manoeuvres,
September 1911.

12in guns, while Germany's
equivalents had four 28cm
(11in) guns. Thus, the new
design could fire a far greater
weight of shells. Fire control
was also improved by doing
away with the medium guns
carried by pre-dreadnoughts.

The extra weight of the big
guns, coupled with armour that
matched that of existing battleships, made *Dreadnought* much
larger than its antecedents, yet
its performance was superior. It
had a top speed of 22 knots, at
least 2 knots better than most
pre-dreadnoughts, and a 30 per
cent longer range, due to the
use, for the first time in a battleship, of steam turbines.

BATTLESHIP BUILDING

It was hardly surprising that the
appearance of *Dreadnought* soon
sparked a naval arms race
between Britain and Germany.
The Royal Navy launched an

additional 23 dreadnoughts
between 1909 and 1914 (with a
further 11 during the war) while
the Germans completed 17 in
the same period and a further 2
during the conflict. Other major
naval powers undertook similar
building programmes – France
laid down 7 in 1912–14, Italy 6
in 1912–15 and the United
States 12 in 1909–15. Later
types were even more powerful
than the original and were
known as super-dreadnoughts.

Clashes between rival fleets
of dreadnoughts were rare with
the Battle of Jutland in 1916

being the only example.
Sinkings were also few and far
between. Germany did not lose
any to enemy action. Britain lost
two: *Audacious* sank after hitting
a German mine in October 1914
and *Vanguard* succumbed to an
internal explosion at Scapa Flow
in 1917.

ADMIRAL JOHN FISHER

Fisher (1841–1920) is rightly
regarded as one of the tower-
ing figures in the history of
the Royal Navy. He was made
First Sea Lord in 1903 and set
in train a vast modernization
programme that included
such new technologies as aircraft and submarines. His
main focus was on surface
warships, however. Here
Fisher created two entirely
new classes – the dread-
nought battleship and the
battle-cruiser. He did much to
prepare the Royal Navy for
war with Germany. He retired
in 1910, returned as First Sea
Lord in 1914 but then
resigned the following year
after quarrelling with Churchill
over the Gallipoli campaign.

Above: The aft 15in (380mm) guns of HMS *Queen Elizabeth*. The Queen
Elizabeth class were the most effective British dreadnoughts of the war.

The Rise of the U-boats

Germany initially relied on various surface warships to sever Britain's maritime trading links but these were increasingly superseded by the far deadlier U-boats that proved highly elusive and difficult to destroy in the first years of the war.

As most of its surface commerce raiders were swept from the high seas during 1914–15, the Imperial German Navy henceforth had to rely almost entirely on its submarines to attack Britain's maritime trade. U-boats had achieved little in 1914 but they were credited with sinking 396 of the 468 Allied or neutral ships lost the following year. Many senior German officers had been sceptical about their value but such results proved their worth. There were more and more coming off the slipways of Germany's naval yards so their campaign could undoubtedly be intensified in 1916.

Yet the senior figures in Germany's military and political circles were engaged in a struggle over naval strategy, chiefly whether U-boats should be allowed to "sink on sight" any ships they encountered, combatant or not. Some, mainly

senior admirals, favoured a return to the strategy of unrestricted submarine warfare, which had been practised for seven months or so in 1915, hoping it would bring Britain to its knees quickly before the British naval blockade did the same to Germany. Others, mostly civilian politicians and diplomats, were more cautious, fearing that a renewal of such a campaign would ultimately bring the United States into the war on the side of the Allies.

NEW PLANS

A compromise of sorts was reached. It was decided that only enemy freighters inside the war zone around the British Isles would be sunk without notice and such ships spotted outside the zone would only be sunk without warning if they were armed. Passenger liners would not be touched in either case. The compromise strategy was announced to the wider world on 11 February 1916 and came into operation on the 29th. The controversial decision proved too much for the head of the Imperial Navy, Admiral Alfred von Tirpitz, and he resigned on 29 March.

The new regulations were soon found wanting. *U-29* spotted the British *Sussex* as it was crossing the English Channel on 24 March and, mistaking the passenger steamer for a troopship, sank it. Three US citizens were among the 50 dead and the

---

U-BOAT ACES

Although underwater warfare was in its infancy in World War I, some U-boat commanders were able to sink a considerable tonnage of Allied ships. Five captains sank more than 210,000 tons of merchant ships and warships but one of them stands head and shoulders above the rest and remains the most successful submarine ace of all time. Lothar von Arnauld de la Périère, captain first of *U-35* and later *U-139*, sank 196 ships of 456,216 tons, almost all of them by gunfire not torpedoes, around a sixth of the total sunk in the war by the whole U-boat force.

Below: A U-boat closes in on one of its victims – a British merchant ship, probably sunk by gunfire.

United States forcefully demanded that Germany end its "present method of submarine warfare" or face a total break in diplomatic relations. The U-boats were ordered to halt their modified unrestricted campaign on 24 April but the sinkings of other targets continued. They scored a notable success on 5 June when the British armoured cruiser HMS *Hampshire* struck a mine laid by a submarine off the Orkneys. The warship sank within minutes, taking with it the country's Minister of War, Field Marshal Horatio Kitchener, who was setting out on a mission to Russia.

YET MORE SINKINGS

Despite the debate over unrestricted warfare, the U-boats had undoubtedly proved themselves in 1916 and the number of their successes had risen enormously. Some 1,157 Allied and neutral ships, including 396 British vessels, had been sunk and 964 of them were directly attributable to German submarines. Mines, some if not quite all laid by U-boats, accounted for a further 161,

Above: HMS *Hampshire* was sunk by a mine laid by *U-75*. Only 12 of those aboard survived.

while surface warships managed just 32 sinkings. Twenty-two boats had been lost but 108 had been commissioned during the year and there were 149 available for action at the beginning of 1917. The clamour for a full return to unrestricted warfare had also been growing. Field Marshal Paul von Hindenburg and his deputy, General Erich Ludendorff, the senior officers who were effectively running Germany's war effort, had demanded as much on 31 August during a meeting with Emperor Wilhelm II.

LT-CDR LOTHAR VON ARNAULD DE LA PÉRIÈRE

A German U-boat captain, de la Périère remains the most successful submarine captain of all time. He led two submarines into action during the war, *U-35* and *U-139*, and in a total of ten cruises in the Mediterranean, sank a staggering 194 merchant vessels and 2 warships. *U-35* was also the top-scoring boat of the war, with a grand total of 224 sinkings to its credit.

Above: De la Périère's *U-35* (nearer) makes a rendezvous with another German submarine, *U-42*.

Left: An Allied steamer begins its final plunge to the bottom after a torpedo strike.

Destroyers

Small, fast destroyers were the workhorses of the rival fleets during the war and were arguably the most important surface warships to see service during the war, protecting battlefleets and merchant ships against submarine and surface attacks.

Scores of destroyers were available to all the major navies in 1914, but they were often in short supply once hostilities had begun. Britain had around 300 and Germany 144, but even a lesser navy like that of Austria-Hungary could call on 25. The various navies had major building programmes in the war – Germany managed to construct 107 but this figure was dwarfed by the 329 completed by the British. They served in a variety of roles but had originally been designed to protect larger warships from attacks by torpedo-boats and were therefore often referred to as "torpedo-boat destroyers" in the early days. They continued this task during 1914–18 but anti-submarine operations gradually became their main priority.

DESTROYER DESIGNS

There were two main types of destroyer in service at the outbreak of war. All generally had a top speed of 25–35 knots. A sizeable number were designed for deep-water operations with the main fleets and so sacrificed some speed for endurance. These types largely equipped the British and German navies. Several powers, such as Austria-Hungary and Italy, built smaller destroyers for short-range work in the calmer and more confined waters of the Mediterranean. For example, the Italian Navy's *Astore*, launched in 1907, had a cruising range of 3,335km (1,800 nautical miles) while the British *Gadfly*, commissioned a year earlier and twice as large, had an endurance of 4,075km (2,200 nautical miles).

Whatever the case, destroyers were generally small enough to be built in quantity by the major navies and inexpensive enough to be bought or constructed by second-rank navies. There were many types of destroyer classes in service but most displaced 500–1,200 tons, had crews of between 80 and 150 and carried a mixture of guns and torpedo-launchers.

ROLES IN ACTION

They generally operated in groups of between 4 and 10 but some flotillas had as many as 20 destroyers. Those flotillas attached to the main fleet were usually commanded from a

---

GERMAN DESTROYERS

The German Navy, like its rivals, used destroyers for a whole range of missions, not least as the eyes of the main battlefleet. Several classes were built in the pre-war period and rather than being given names they had letter and numerical designations, the letter reflecting the maker. Thus G was the Germania shipyard, S Schichau and V Vulcan, for example.

TYPE: G40 destroyer
LAID DOWN: 1914
DISPLACEMENT: 1,050 tons
CREW: 87
SPEED: 34.5 knots
MAIN ARMAMENT: 3 x 8.5cm (3.3in) guns; 6 x 50.8cm (20in) torpedo tubes

Below: The end of the road for the German destroyer flotillas – interned in Scapa Flow in 1918.

Right: A flotilla of British
destroyers sailing in line ahead, part
of the Harwich Force that was active
in the southern North Sea.

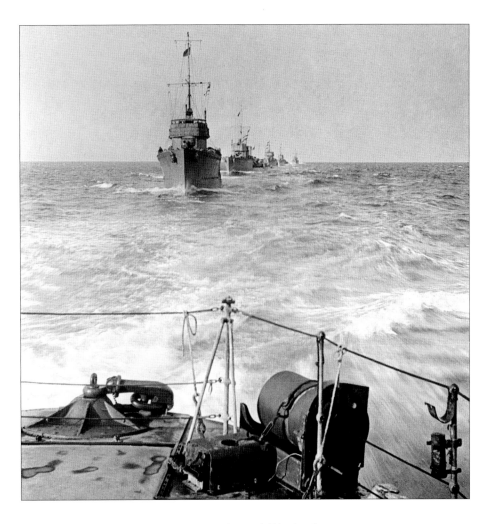

larger warship, such as a light cruiser, and had several roles. They acted as fast scouts, prevented enemy surface ships or submarines from launching torpedo attacks against larger warships, and used their own torpedoes if the opportunity presented itself. Destroyers were indispensable and no main fleet would go to sea without their protective screen. The British committed 73 destroyers to the Battle of Jutland in 1916 while Germany had 61 present.

Destroyers did not just operate with the main fleets and had two main roles when acting independently. First there was coastal defence, stopping raids by rival destroyers against inshore maritime trade routes and ports. Second, and more importantly for the Allies, destroyers were the cornerstone of the anti-submarine warfare campaign against Germany's U-boats. These operations required types with greater range and endurance and later Allied destroyers were something like twice the size of earlier classes. Britain's W class, which appeared in 1917–18, had a displacement of 1,529 tons and an endurance of 6,430km (3,470 nautical miles).

Much of the destroyers' everyday work went unsung but because of their general ubiquity they also suffered considerably. The Allies lost 112 to all causes of which more than 50 per cent were British as the Royal Navy bore the brunt of the anti-submarine campaign. The Central Powers lost 62 destroyers in total of which 53 were German.

Left: HMS *Windsor*, like other British V and W class destroyers, was armed with 4 x 4in (101mm) guns and served on into WWII.

Torpedo-boats

Torpedoes were deadly weapons that allowed small, fast warships to pack a considerable punch. Torpedo-boats' main targets were meant to be the enemy fleets of old battleships and more modern dreadnoughts.

These light and speedy boats were the first warships to be armed with torpedoes, a weapon that was developed in the late 19th century. Torpedo-boats caused alarm in some naval circles when they first appeared, mainly because they gave the smallest navy a chance to sink the biggest battleships for little financial outlay. As the boats were so relatively cheap to produce, a country with a small defence budget could buy or build dozens of them.

Most navies had flotillas of torpedo-boats at the outbreak of World War I and they came in two main categories. Some boats were smaller, with only a limited range and were used in coastal waters, while other types were built for longer patrols and

Above: Ships of France's Arquebuse class in port at Toulon.

more distant operations. The latter were increasingly being superseded by destroyers, bigger and faster warships that also carried torpedoes.

The coastal boats tended to be armed solely with torpedoes, although some were fitted with machine-guns. Speed rather than defensive armament was usually their best chance of survival. If they were sent on longer-range missions, coastal torpedo-boats were usually towed to their target area but some were also deployed from the decks of a class of support vessels generally known as torpedo depot ships.

MAS BOATS IN ACTION

The Italian Navy operated the most successful coastal torpedo-boats and was the acknowledged world leader in their design at the start of the war. One of the leading producers was the Società Veneziana Automobili Nautiche (SVAN). Their 16-ton MAS (Motobarca Armata SVAN) boats waged a highly effective hit-and-run

Below: Sleek German torpedo boats pictured at anchor in the Kiel Canal in January 1914.

campaign across the Adriatic Sea during 1915–18. The boats became so successful and renowned for their exploits that the nationalist writer Gabriele d'Annunzio gave them a slogan which translates as "One against a hundred – Attack!"

The MAS boats often operated at night and their most spectacular feat of arms came on 10 June 1918, when a pair of them attacked the Austro-Hungarian dreadnought *Szent István* off Premuda Island in the northern Adriatic at around 03.00 hours and one of them, *MAS 15* captained by Commander Luigi Rizzo, scored a fatal torpedo hit. The dreadnought sank some three hours later and its loss was so psychologically damaging that the main Austro-Hungarian fleet never put to sea again. The attack was Rizzo's second major success of the war as his *MAS 9* had sunk the old Austro-Hungarian battleship *Wien* in Muggia Bay near Trieste on 9 December the previous year.

BALTIC OPERATIONS

The other major actions involving coastal motor boats (CMBs) actually came some months after the end of the war, when British forces stationed in Russia became embroiled in the ongoing civil war. British torpedo-boats were based on the coast of newly independent Finland and they undertook two highly successful raids against Bolshevik targets. The three-man *CMB4*, commanded by Lieutenant Augustine Agar,

Right: Destroyers originally evolved to take on smaller torpedo-boats like these French types seen docked at Le Havre in 1913.

BRITISH *CMB65A*

Britain developed a number of Coastal Motor Boats, mostly designed by the Thornycroft firm. They came in three types, ranging in length from 12–21m (40–70ft). The torpedoes were fired backwards out of the boat from troughs and the boats had to swerve away quickly to avoid being hit.

DISPLACEMENT: 10 tons
LENGTH: 16.7m (55ft)
ENGINE: 350hp Thornycroft Y type
TOP SPEED: 35 knots+
CREW: 3
ARMAMENT: 1 or 2 x 18in (457mm) torpedo tubes; 2–4 machine-guns

sank the cruiser *Oleg* in Kronstadt harbour on 17 June 1919. Their greatest exploit came early on the morning of 19 August, when seven CMBs led by Commander Claude Dobson again broke into the heavily defended harbour at Kronstadt. For the loss of three of his small boats, Dobson's flotilla sank the armoured cruiser *Pamiat Azova* and the dreadnought *Petropavlovsk*, and badly damaged the battleship *Andrei Pervozvanni*.

Allied Submarines

*Although the German U-boat fleet grabbed the headlines during World War I,
the Allied navies also deployed their own flotillas of submarines and, even if they
were not so spectacularly successful, they played their own part in the final victory.*

All the main Allied nations deployed submarines during World War I. In 1914 France had the biggest fleet of all, 123 boats. Italy had 25 mostly short-range types in service and Russia had 41. Few boats were built during the war, just 25 in France, 46 in Italy and 40 in Russia. France's existing types were old and unreliable, Italy's were beset by logistical problems, and Russian submarines were outdated, although they did operate in the Baltic and Black Seas. French, Italian and Russian losses totalled 12, 8 and 20 respectively.

Right: British submarine crewmen stand watch protected from the elements by nothing more than a canvas screen.

Although the British did not have the world's largest fleet of submarines in 1914, they had its largest and most successful one by the Armistice. Some 17 D- and E-class boats were available in August 1914 and these were backed by 40 B- and C-class types that were considered fit only for coastal operations. By the Armistice the numbers had swelled to 137 on active service with a further 78 under construction; 54 were lost during the conflict.

BRITISH ACTIONS

The British produced a number of different types but the mainstay were the E-class boats that were active particularly in the Baltic Sea and Dardanelles. Fifty-eight were built from 1913–17 and 22 were lost. The first pair sailed for the Baltic during October 1914, largely to help the Russians as their modern submarines were being crippled by a lack of (German-built) engines. A further four E-class boats reached the Baltic in 1915 and were joined by four C-class types that had been taken apart, carried by ship to Archangel and then transported by rail and barge to the Gulf of Finland where they were then reassembled.

The British submarines sank a number of warships but their greatest contribution to the war effort was to hunt down German freighters transporting Swedish iron ore down the Gulf

---

BRITISH K-CLASS SUBMARINES

These large submarines (the conning tower and some crew members of *K-6* are shown) were designed to operate with the main surface warships of the Royal Navy but the general concept was flawed, not least because they took an age to submerge as the funnels for their steam turbines had to be made watertight. Collisions with large vessels and even their own kind were not uncommon and 5 of the 17 built before 1919 were lost in accidents.

DISPLACEMENT: 2,140 tons (surface)
CREW: 50–60
RANGE: 5,555km (3,000nm)
ARMAMENT: 10 x 21in (533mm) torpedo tubes; 3 x 4in (102mm) guns

---

of Bothnia. This campaign ended with the signing of the Treaty of Brest-Litovsk in March 1918. Under its terms the Germans demanded that the Bolsheviks give up the British submarines. Rather than surrender, the final seven sailed from Helsingfors (Helsinki) on 8 April and their crews scuttled them in deep water.

IN THE MEDITERRANEAN

The Dardanelles campaign in 1915 again involved a number of E-class boats. They crippled the Turkish merchant fleet plying the Sea of Marmara, bombarded various shore installations, and even reached Constantinople. One boat, *E-11* captained by Lieutenant-Commander Martin Nasmith, was particularly successful, sinking 27 steamers and 58 other vessels in three patrols. The campaign netted 2 battleships, 1 destroyer, 5 gunboats, 7 supply ships, 9 troop transports, 35 steamers and 188 other

HMS *E-11*

The British submarine *E-11*, seen here after sailing through the Turkish-controlled Dardanelles, served with great distinction in the Sea of Marmara in 1915, even sinking a Turkish vessel at anchor in Constantinople's Golden Horn on 23 May. In all, 58 E-class boats were built and these also served in the North Sea and Baltic; 22 were lost.

DISPLACEMENT: 667 tons
CREW: 30
RANGE: 6,655km (3,600nm)
ARMAMENT: 5 x 18in (457mm) torpedo tubes; 1 x 12pdr (76mm) gun

vessels. Four boats were sunk while trying to pass through the Dardanelles; 9 reached the Sea of Marmara and 3 were lost in action there.

The E class was a reliable design but the British also experimented with one of the worst submarines of the war, the steam-driven K class. These were huge boats developed to serve with the Grand Fleet rather than operate as lone hunters. Friendly warships had difficulty in detecting them on the surface in anything but dead calm conditions and the submarines themselves took an age to dive. Collisions and accidents were inevitable, as became clear during an exercise off the Scottish coast on the night of 31 January 1918. *K-4* was sunk by *K-6* and *K-17* was despatched by a British cruiser in the so-called "Battle of May Island".

Below: The French submarine *Diane* was lost to an unexplained internal explosion in March 1918.

Anti-submarine Weapons

In 1914 no weapons existed that could destroy a submerged submarine but the dangers posed by Germany's U-boats forced the Allies – and especially Britain – to develop a range of passive and aggressive techniques to combat this new menace.

Anti-submarine warfare was very much in its infancy at the outbreak of World War I as most navies had focused their energies on developing offensive surface technologies in previous years. The need to combat submarines became apparent in the first weeks of the conflict and was felt most acutely by the British as their crucial maritime trade and large merchant fleet bore the brunt of Germany's U-boat campaign.

PASSIVE DEFENCES

At first the best defence for vessels, both warships and freighters, was speed and zig-zagging as U-boats were very slow both submerged and on the surface and found it difficult to hit targets that were changing course regularly. Ships sailing at night or ones that avoided busy sea lanes also stood a better chance of survival. Next came complex camouflage of the "dazzle" type that covered ships in geometrical patterns of paint to break up their outline. Warships at anchor were often protected by anti-submarine nets that were let down over their sides on booms to stop torpedoes but these were found too cumbersome and of little value. Larger anti-submarine barrages – combinations of nets, minefields and patrolling war-

Above: One of the first successful depth-charge launchers stands ready for action.

ships – were also devised to protect narrow stretches of sea and vulnerable routes, such as the English Channel, but they were far from impervious.

Warships in 1914 could only sink surfaced submarines and then only by ramming or gun-

fire, while submerged U-boats were effectively invulnerable. For much of the war U-boat captains liked to use gunfire to sink unarmed targets rather than waste torpedoes, so the Allies responded by fitting weapons to merchant vessels. The British also created Q-ships, seemingly unarmed vessels that invited attack on the surface at close range but which actually carried an array of hidden weapons. These were not as successful as hoped and submariners became wary of approaching too close to any likely Q-ship.

The British also developed a system in which a potential target towed a friendly submerged submarine. If a U-boat attacked on the surface, the surface ship could telephone the submerged submarine by a line attached to the tow rope

Right: Q-ships like this were a British invention designed to lure U-boats into a surface attack.

Q-ships were innocent-looking civilian vessels given hidden armament

The Royal Navy eventually deployed some 366 Q-ships; they sank 11 U-boats but 61 were lost in action

Sometimes their holds were filled with wood so that they would stay afloat longer if hit below the waterline and its captain would then slip the rope and manoeuvre into a position to attack the U-boat.

NEW WEAPONS

There were other new means of attacking targets. British destroyers towed electronically detonated charges (sweeps) behind them but these needed very close contact to sink a submarine. Depth charges (bombs designed to explode under water) became available in late 1915 but only appeared in quantity from 1917 onward. Hydrophones, directional underwater microphones for listening to U-boat engines, were developed but submariners learned to outfox them by diving deep or by silent running. The first successful attack using both hydrophones and depth charges took place on 16 July 1916. Other means of locating submarines included intercepting their radio messages and using various aircraft and airships to find them on the surface.

Some 178 German U-boats were lost during 1914–18; 38 were sunk in accidents or for some other unknown reason. Of the remaining 140, 50 were sunk by mines, 29 by depth charges, 19 by gunfire, 19 by ramming, 18 by torpedo and 1 in an air attack. The most lethal areas were the waters immediately around the British Isles and the near North Atlantic, where 90 and 44 U-boats were lost, respectively. Most sinkings occurred after convoys were introduced in April 1917.

Above: US troopships head for Europe. The convoy system was so successful that not one troopship carrying the US Army to France was lost to a U-boat attack.

THE SPIDER'S WEB

Mathematical methods were used to develop a pattern of anti-submarine patrols to be conducted by British naval aircraft over the North Sea. A mixture of Curtiss H-12 and Felixstowe flying boats began flying an octagonal pattern of patrol lines from May 1917. and these were calculated to allow just four flying boats to cover some 10,000 sq km (3,860 sq miles) in a mere five hours. The patrols were over routes known to be taken by surfaced U-boats. The British claimed their first success on the 20th and several other kills were recorded. Though these were unconfirmed the web certainly made life more difficult for the U-boats and their crews.

Left: Part of an Allied convoy arrives at an unspecified port. Note the dazzle camouflage pattern.

Cruisers

Cruisers were a key component of all of the world's major navies during World War I and they were capable of operating both independently, often far from home waters, or as part of the main battlefleet in large-scale actions.

Cruisers were originally developed by the British Royal Navy in the latter part of the 19th century. They were smaller than existing battleships but faster and still able to undertake long-range, ocean missions. There were originally two types of cruisers. Armoured cruisers were deployed as scout warships with the main battlefleet and had large-calibre armaments and significant side armour. Protected cruisers dispensed with the thick side armour but did have some deck armour. These types mainly operated in defence of trade routes or foreign naval stations, or formed the core of the squadrons deployed to defend imperial possessions. All of the combatant nations had cruisers of one type or another by the outbreak of war – for the Allies France had 37 and Russia 15,

Above: HMS *Warrior* was the lead vessel in a class of four armoured cruisers but was lost at Jutland.

Below: Germany's *Goeben*, a battle-cruiser, leads *Breslau*, one of a class of four light cruisers completed in 1912, out to sea.

while for the Central Powers, Germany had 52 and Austria-Hungary 9.

CRUISER ROLES

Britain had a large force of armoured cruisers in 1914, around 40, but they had in fact been made largely redundant in the scouting role with the main fleet thanks to the development of the dreadnought battle-cruiser, the first of which was launched in 1908. Britain also had some 100 protected cruisers on the eve of war but these increasingly gave way to lighter, faster types. Germany's heavier cruisers were largely relegated to secondary duties by the outbreak of war and its main High Seas Fleet relied mostly on light cruisers. The distinction between armoured and protected cruisers and light cruisers was quite stark. The last were roughly half the displacement, had a high speed and carried guns of much smaller calibre.

Nevertheless, both of the original types continued to see action. The British deployed them to hunt down Germany's surface raiders and sent them overseas where they formed the heart of the local squadrons, often along with older pre-dreadnought battleships. From 1917 onward they were also used nearer home as convoy escorts. Germany, in contrast, used many of its light cruisers to harry Allied shipping lanes and merchant ships in the first few months of the war before they were largely hunted down, although light cruisers also saw action with the country's main battlefleet.

LOSSES IN COMBAT

Cruisers were therefore present at many major naval battles during the war. There were 13 British and German warships present at the Battle of the Falklands in late 1914, for example, and all but three, all

British, were either armoured or light cruisers. Similarly, there were numerous cruisers at the biggest naval engagement of the war, the Battle of Jutland in 1916. The various parts of Britain's Grand Fleet mustered 8 armoured and 26 light cruisers while Germany's High Seas Fleet had 11 light cruisers.

Cruisers were potentially highly vulnerable in battles involving larger warships and this certainly proved to be the case at Jutland. Germany lost four light cruisers, including the *Rostock*, which had to be scuttled after suffering heavy damage from a torpedo fired by a British destroyer, and *Wiesbaden*, which went to the bottom after receiving multiple shell hits. *Elbing* and *Frauenlob* were also sunk by torpedoes. The Grand Fleet lost three of its armoured cruisers, *Black Prince*, *Defence* and *Warrior*, to gunfire from larger warships.

The Allies lost a total of 39 cruisers of all types during the war, while the Central Powers lost 28 to various causes.

LÉON GAMBETTA

The French armoured cruiser *Léon Gambetta* was largely designed for coastal defence and the protection of trade routes and was unfit to serve with the main fleet in large-scale actions, as even by contemporary standards it was slow and poorly armed. The *Léon Gambetta* was sunk in the Gulf of Otranto on the night of 24 April 1915, victim of a torpedo fired by the Austro-Hungarian submarine *U-5* (captained by top Austrian U-boat ace Georg Trapp, later made famous by the musical *The Sound of Music*).

LAID DOWN: 1901
DISPLACEMENT: 12,250 tons
CREW: 734
SPEED: 22 knots
MAIN ARMAMENT: 4 x 194mm (7.6in) and 16 x 164.7mm (6.4in) guns

HMS *BLACK PRINCE*

This British armoured cruiser was launched in 1907 and was stationed in the Mediterranean in 1914. It then served with the Grand Fleet's 1st Cruiser Squadron. During the Battle of Jutland in 1916 *Black Prince* was hit by 21 German shells, 15 of them from heavy guns, and sank with all hands.

LAID DOWN: 1903
DISPLACEMENT: 13,550 tons

CREW: 857
SPEED: 23 knots
MAIN ARMAMENT: 6 x 9.2in (234mm) and 10 x 6in (152mm) guns

Index